MERCURY
READER

a custom publication

Thomas Nicholas

Lansing Community College

Pearson Custom Publishing

New York   Boston   San Francisco
London   Toronto   Sydney   Tokyo   Singapore   Madrid
Mexico City   Munich   Paris   Cape Town   Hong Kong   Montreal

Senior Vice President, Editorial and Marketing: Patrick F. Boles
Senior Sponsoring Editor: Natalie Danner
Development Editors: Mary Kate Paris and Katherine R. Gehan
Editorial Assistant: Jill Johnson
Operations Manager: Eric M. Kenney
Database Product Manager: Jennifer Berry
Rights Manager: Katie Huha
Art Director: Renée Sartell
Cover Designers: Renée Sartell and Sharon Treacy

Cover Art: "Gigantia Mountains & Sea of Cortes," by R.G.K. Photography, Copyright © Tony Stone Images; "Dime," courtesy of the Shaw Collection.

Please visit our websites at *www.pearsoncustom.com* and *www.mercuryreader.com.*

Attention bookstores: For permission to return any unsold stock, contact us at *pe-uscustomreturns@pearson.com.*

**Pearson
Custom Publishing**
is a division of

www.pearsonhighered.com

ISBN 10: 0-536-79199-6
ISBN 13: 978-0-536-79199-3

Contents

I

LOVE AND LOSS

EDUCATION AND LEARNING

Growing Up

Russell Baker

Russell Baker (1925–) was born in a rural town in Virginia and grew up in New Jersey and Maryland. He received his B. A. in English from Johns Hopkins University in 1947 and worked as a reporter for the Baltimore Sun *and then the* New York Times. *In 1962 he began writing his "Observer" column for the* Times, *which was syndicated in over 400 newspapers for more than two decades. His topics range from the mundane everyday annoyances to serious social problems, and his style is generally casual but thoughtful. In 1979 he received the Pulitzer Prize for distinguished commentary; he received the Prize again for his autobiography* Growing Up *(1982), from which the following selection is excerpted. His collections of columns and essays include* All Things Considered *(1965),* Poor Russell's Almanac *(1972),* So This Is Depravity *(1980)* The Rescue of Miss Yaskell and Other Pipe Dreams *(1983), and* There's a Country in My Cellar *(1990). The following excerpt from his autobiography describes, with humor and insight, the moment when he decides he wants to become a writer.*

1   I began working in journalism when I was eight years old. It was my mother's idea. She wanted me to "make something" of myself and, after a levelheaded appraisal of my strengths, decided I had better start young if I was to have any chance of keeping up with the competition.

     The flaw in my character which she had already spotted was lack of "gumption." My idea of a perfect afternoon was lying in front of the radio rereading my favorite Big Little Book, *Dick Tracy Meets*

Stooge Viller. My mother despised inactivity. Seeing me having a good time in repose, she was powerless to hide her disgust. "You've got no more gumption than a bump on a log," she said. "Get out in the kitchen and help Doris do those dirty dishes."

My sister Doris, though two years younger than I, had enough gumption for a dozen people. She positively enjoyed washing dishes, making beds, and cleaning the house. When she was only seven she could carry a piece of short-weighted cheese back to the A&P, threaten the manager with legal action, and come back triumphantly with the full quarter-pound we'd paid for and a few ounces extra thrown in for forgiveness. Doris could have made something of herself if she hadn't been a girl. Because of this defect, however, the best she could hope for was a career as a nurse or schoolteacher, the only work that capable females were considered up to. in those days.

This must have saddened my mother, this twist of fate that had allocated all the gumption to the daughter and left her with a son who was content with Dick Tracy and Stooge Viller. If disappointed, though, she wasted no energy on self-pity. She would make me make something of myself whether I wanted to or not. "The Lord helps those who help themselves," she said. That was the way her mind worked.

She was realistic about the difficulty. Having sized up the material the Lord had given her to mold, she didn't overestimate what she could do with it. She didn't insist that I grow up to be President of the United States.

Fifty years ago parents still asked boys if they wanted to grow up to be President, and asked it not jokingly but seriously. Many parents who were hardly more than paupers still believed their sons could do it. Abraham Lincoln had done it. We were only sixty-five years from Lincoln. Many a grandfather who walked among us could remember Lincoln's time. Men of grandfatherly age were the worst for asking if you wanted to grow up to be President. A surprising number of little boys said yes and meant it.

I was asked many times myself. No, I would say, I didn't want to grow up to be President. My mother was present during one of these interrogations. An elderly uncle, having posed the usual question and exposed my lack of interest in the Presidency, asked, "Well, what *do* you want to be when you grow up?"

I loved to pick through trash piles and collect empty bottles, tin cans with pretty labels, and discarded magazines. The most desirable job on earth sprang instantly to mind. "I want to be a garbage man," I said.

My uncle smiled, but my mother had seen the first distressing evidence of a bump budding on a log. "Have a little gumption, Russell," she said. Her calling me Russell was a signal of unhappiness. When she approved of me I was always "Buddy."

10 When I turned eight years old she decided that the job of starting me on the road toward making something of myself could no longer be safely delayed. "Buddy," she said one day, "I want you to come home right after school this afternoon. Somebody's coming and I want you to meet him."

When I burst in that afternoon she was in conference in the parlor with an executive of the Curtis Publishing Company. She introduced me. He bent low from the waist and shook my hand. Was it true as my mother had told him, he asked, that I longed for the opportunity to conquer the world of business?

My mother replied that I was blessed with a rare determination to make something of myself.

"That's right," I whispered.

"But have you got the grit, the character, the never-say-quit spirit it takes to succeed in business?"

15 My mother said I certainly did.

"That's right," I said.

He eyed me silently for a long pause, as though weighing whether I could be trusted to keep his confidence, then spoke man-to-man. Before taking a crucial step, he said, he wanted to advise me that working for the Curtis Publishing Company placed enormous responsibility on a young man. It was one of the great companies of America. Perhaps the greatest publishing house in the world. I had heard, no doubt, of the *Saturday Evening Post?*

Heard of it? My mother said that everyone in our house had heard of the *Saturday Post* and that I, in fact, read it with religious devotion.

Then doubtless he said, we were also familiar with those two monthly pillars of the magazine world, the *Ladies Home Journal* and the *Country Gentleman.*

20 Indeed we were familiar with them, said my mother.

Representing the *Saturday Evening Post* was one of the weightiest honors that could be bestowed in the world of business, he said. He was personally proud of being a part of that great corporation.

My mother said he had every right to be.

Again he studied me as though debating whether I was worthy of a knighthood. Finally: "Are you trustworthy?"

My mother said I was the soul of honesty.

"That's right," I said.

The caller smiled for the first time. He told me I was a lucky young man. He admired my spunk. Too many young men thought life was all play. Those young men would not go far in this world. Only a young man willing to work and save and keep his face washed and his hair neatly combed could hope to come out on top in a world such as ours. Did I truly and sincerely believe that I was such a young man?

"He certainly does," said my mother.

"That's right," I said.

He said he had been so impressed by what he had seen of me that he was going to make me a representative of the Curtis Publishing Company. On the following Tuesday, he said, thirty freshly printed copies of the *Saturday Evening Post* would be delivered at our door. I would place these magazines, still damp with the ink of the presses, in a handsome canvas bag, sling it over my shoulder, and set forth through the streets to bring the best in journalism, fiction, and cartoons to the American public.

He had brought the canvas bag with him. He presented it with reverence fit for a chasuble. He showed me how to drape the sling over my left shoulder and across the chest so that the pouch lay easily accessible to my right hand, allowing the best in journalism, fiction, and cartoons to be swiftly extracted and sold to a citizenry whose happiness and security depended upon us soldiers of the free press.

The following Tuesday I raced home from school, put the canvas bag over my shoulder, dumped the magazines in, and, tilting to the left to balance their weight on my right hip, embarked on the highway of journalism.

We lived in Belleville, New Jersey, a commuter town at the northern fringe of Newark. It was 1932, the bleakest year of the Depression. My father had died two years before, leaving us with a few pieces of Sears, Roebuck furniture and not much else, and my mother had taken Doris and me to live with one of her younger brothers. This was my Uncle Allen. Uncle Allen had made something of himself by 1932.

4

As salesman for a soft-drink bottler in Newark, he had an income of $30 a week; wore pearl-gray spats, detachable collars, and a three-piece suit; was happily married; and took in threadbare relatives.

With my load of magazines I headed toward Belleville Avenue. That's where the people were. There were two filling stations at the intersection with Union Avenue, as well as an A&P, a fruit stand, a bakery, a barber shop, Zuccarelli's drugstore, and a diner shaped like a railroad car. For several hours I made myself highly visible, shifting position now and then from corner to corner, from shop window to shop window, to make sure everyone could see the heavy black lettering on the canvas bag that said THE SATURDAY EVENING POST. When the angle of the light indicated it was suppertime, I walked back to the house.

"How many did you sell, Buddy?" my mother asked.

35 "None." 35

"Where did you go?"

"The corner of Belleville and Union Avenues."

"What did you do?"

"Stood on the corner waiting for somebody to buy a *Saturday Evening Post.*"

40 "You just stood there?" 40

"Didn't sell a single one."

"For God's sake, Russell!"

Uncle Allen intervened. "I've been thinking about it for some time," he said, "and I've about decided to take the *Post* regularly. Put me down as a regular customer." I handed him a magazine and he paid me a nickel. It was the first nickel I earned.

Afterwards my mother instructed me in salesmanship. I would have to ring doorbells, address adults with charming self-confidence, and break down resistance with a sales talk pointing out that no one, no matter how poor, could afford to be without the *Saturday Evening Post* in the home.

45 I told my mother I'd changed my mind about wanting to succeed 45
in the magazine business.

"If you think I'm going to raise a good-for-nothing," she replied, "you've got another think coming." She told me to hit the streets with the canvas bag and start ringing doorbells the instant school was out next day. When I objected that I didn't feel any aptitude for salesmanship, she asked how I'd like to lend her my leather belt so she could whack some sense into me, I bowed to superior will and entered journalism with a heavy heart.

My mother and I had fought this battle almost as long as I could remember. It probably started even before memory began, when I was a country child in northern Virginia and my mother, dissatisfied with my father's plain workman's life, determined that I would not grow up like him and his people, with calluses on their hands, overalls on their backs, and fourth-grade educations in their heads. She had fancier ideas of life's possibilities. Introducing me to the *Saturday Evening Post,* she was trying to wean me as early as possible from my father's world where men left with their lunch pails at sunup, worked with their hands until the grime ate into the pores, and died with a few sticks of mail-order furniture as their legacy. In my mother's vision of the better life there were desks and white collars, well-pressed suits, evenings of reading and lively talk, and perhaps—if a man were very, very lucky and hit the jackpot, really made something important of himself—perhaps there might be a fantastic salary of $5,000 a year to support a big house and a Buick with a rumble seat and a vacation in Atlantic City.

And so I set forth with my sack of magazines. I was afraid of the dogs that snarled behind the doors of potential buyers. I was timid about ringing the doorbells of strangers, relieved when no one came to the door, and scared when someone did. Despite my mother's instructions, I could not deliver an engaging sales pitch. When a door opened I simply asked, "Want to buy a *Saturday Evening Post?*" In Belleville few persons did. It was a town of 30,000 people, and most weeks I rang a fair majority of its doorbells. But I rarely sold my thirty copies. Some weeks I canvassed the entire town for six days and still had four or five unsold magazines on Monday evening; then I dreaded the coming of Tuesday morning, when a batch of thirty fresh *Saturday Evening Post*s was due at the front door.

"Better get out there and sell the rest of those magazines tonight," My mother would say.

I usually posted myself then at a busy intersection where a traffic light controlled commuter flow from Newark. When the light turned red I stood on the curb and shouted my sales pitch at the motorists.

"Want to buy a *Saturday Evening Post?*"

6

One rainy night when car windows were sealed against me I came back soaked and with not a single sale to report. My mother beckoned to Doris.

"Go back down there with Buddy and show him how to sell these magazines," she said.

Brimming with zest, Doris, who was then seven years old, returned with me to the corner. She took a magazine from the bag, and when the light turned red she strode to the nearest car and banged her small fist against the closed window. The driver, probably startled at what he took to be a midget assaulting his car, lowered the window to stare, and Doris thrust a *Saturday Evening Post* at him.

"You need this magazine," she piped, "and it only costs a nickel."

Her salesmanship was irresistible. Before the light changed half a dozen times she disposed of the entire batch. I didn't feel humiliated. To the contrary, I was so happy I decided to give her a treat. Leading her to the vegetable store on Belleville Avenue, I bought three apples, which cost a nickel, and gave her one.

"You shouldn't waste money," she said.

"Eat your apple." I bit into mine.

"You shouldn't eat before supper," she said. "It'll spoil your appetite."

Back at the house that evening, she dutifully reported me for wasting a nickel. Instead of a scolding, I was rewarded with a pat on the back for having the good sense to buy fruit instead of candy. My mother reached into her bottomless supply of maxims and told Doris, "An apple a day keeps the doctor away."

By the time I was ten I had learned all my mother's maxims by heart. Asking to stay up past normal bedtime, I knew that a refusal would be explained with, "Early to bed and early to rise, makes a man healthy, wealthy, and wise." If I whimpered about having to get up early in the morning, I could depend on her to say, "The early bird gets the worm."

The one I most despised was, "If at first you don't succeed, try, try again." This was the battle cry with which she constantly sent me back into the hopeless struggle whenever I moaned that I had rung every doorbell in town and knew there wasn't a single potential buyer left in Belleville that week. After listening to my explanation, she handed me the canvas bag and said, "If at first you don't succeed . . . "

Three years in that job, which I would gladly have quit after the first day except for her insistence, produced at least one valuable result. My mother finally concluded that I would never make something of myself by pursuing a life in business and started considering careers that demanded less competitive zeal.

One evening when I was eleven I brought home a short "composition" on my summer vacation which the teacher had graded with an A. Reading it with her own schoolteacher's eye, my mother agreed that it was top-drawer seventh grade prose and complimented me. Nothing more was said about it immediately, but a new idea had taken life in her mind. Halfway through supper she suddenly interrupted the conversation.

"Buddy," she said, "maybe you could be a writer."

I clasped the idea to my heart. I had never met a writer, had shown no previous urge to write, and hadn't a notion how to become a writer, but I loved stories and thought that making up stories must surely be almost as much fun as reading them. Best of all, though, and what really gladdened my heart, was the ease of the writer's life. Writers did not have to trudge through the town peddling from canvas bags, defending themselves against angry dogs, being rejected by surly strangers. Writers did not have to ring doorbells. So far as I could make out, what writers did couldn't even be classified as work.

I was enchanted. Writers didn't have to have any gumption at all. I did not dare tell anybody for fear of being laughed at in the schoolyard, but secretly I decided that what I'd like to be when I grew up was a writer.

Questions on Meaning

1. What does Baker mean by "gumption"? How does he use that word throughout this story to classify activities he doesn't like, just as he wants to be a writer because it does not require having gumption?
2. How would you characterize Baker's relationship with his mother? His sister? What descriptions in the narrative give you that impression?
3. Do you agree with Baker's assessment of writing: "what writers did couldn't even be classified as work"? In what sense, to him at least, is it *not* work?

Questions on Rhetorical Strategy and Style

1. Describe the tone of this story. Identify some of the language Baker uses that reveals his attitude toward his subject.
2. This section of Baker's autobiography is mostly written as narration. What specific writing techniques does Baker use to keep us interested?
3. What is the effect of Baker's sense of humor? For example, when he seems to make fun of his mother for having a maxim for every occasion, what is he really satirizing—his mother as a person, or an attitude toward life? What gives you that impression?

Writing Assignments

1. Can you recall when you first decided what you wanted to be when you grew up? What led you to that decision—family members, friends, observations, personal interests? Can you remember the specifics of your thinking at that time—what made you so sure of your decision? Compare that state of mind with your present thoughts about that particular occupation. What is different about how adults think about "work" than how children think of it?
2. Baker's essay supports the truism that one's occupation should ideally fit one's personality. Consider your own plans for a career or profession after you complete your education. Why have you chosen your field of interest? Beyond the concept of finding a certain career "interesting," what personality characteristics do you imagine are most important for someone working day to day in that area? Do you have these characteristics? Write a personal essay exploring and explaining your choice of career in terms of these questions.

What Is Intelligence, Anyway?

Isaac Asimov

Isaac Asimov (1920–1992) was born in Russia but grew up in America. He received his Ph.D. in chemistry from Columbia University and thereafter taught biochemistry. He is better known as a science and science fiction writer. His three Foundation *novels were published in the 1950s, followed by the* Robot *novels and literally dozens of additional novels, collections of short stories, popular science books, and essays. Although educated as a scientific specialist and academician, Asimov always made it his goal to write for nonspecialized readers. He is perhaps best known for his writing—both nonfiction and fiction—that explains scientific concepts and realities for the general public. You will see that quality in this essay, which addresses the question of what intelligence really is. The essay is obviously written for a general reader and avoids technical or scientific discussion of intelligence. This approach has both strengths and weaknesses as Asimov seeks to increase our understanding of the quality of intelligence.*

1   What is intelligence, anyway? When I was in the Army, I received a kind of aptitude test that all soldiers took and, against a normal of 100, scored 160. No one at the base had ever seen a figure like that, and for two hours they made a big fuss over me. (It didn't mean anything. The next day I was still a buck private with KP as my highest duty.)

     All my life I've been registering scores like that, so that I have the complacent feeling that I'm highly intelligent, and I expect other people to think so, too. Actually, though, don't such scores simply mean

Reprinted with the permission of the Estate of Isaac Asimov, c/o Ralph M. Vicinanza, Ltd.

that I am very good at answering the type of academic questions that are considered worthy of answers by the people who make up the intelligence tests—people with intellectual bents similar to mine?

For instance, I had an auto repairman once, who, on these intelligence tests, could not possibly have scored more than 80, by my estimate. I always took it for granted that I was far more intelligent than he was. Yet, when anything went wrong with my car, I hastened to him with it, watched him anxiously as he explored its vitals, and listened to his pronouncements as though they were divine oracles—and he always fixed my car.

Well then, suppose my auto repairman devised questions for an intelligence test. Or suppose a carpenter did, or a farmer, or, indeed, almost anyone but an academician. By every one of those tests, I'd prove myself a moron. And I'd *be* a moron, too. In a world where I could not use my academic training and my verbal talents but had to do something intricate or hard, working with my hands, I would do poorly. My intelligence, then, is not absolute but is a function of the society I live in and of the fact that a small subsection of that society has managed to foist itself on the rest as an arbiter of such matters.

Consider my auto repairman, again. He had a habit of telling me jokes whenever he saw me. One time he raised his head from under the automobile hood to say, "Doc, a deaf-and-dumb guy went into a hardware store to ask for some nails. He put two fingers together on the counter and made hammering motions with the other hand. The clerk brought him a hammer. He shook his head and pointed to the two fingers he was hammering. The clerk brought him nails. He picked out the sizes he wanted, and left. Well, doc, the next guy who came in was a blind man. He wanted scissors. How do you suppose he asked for them?"

Indulgently, I lifted my right hand and made scissoring motions with my first two fingers. Whereupon my auto repairman laughed raucously and said, "Why, you dumb jerk, he used his *voice* and asked for them." Then he said, smugly, "I've been trying that on all my customers today." "Did you catch many?" I asked. "Quite a few," he said, "but I knew for sure I'd catch *you*." "Why is that?" I asked. "Because you're so goddamned educated, doc, I *knew* you couldn't be very smart."

And I have an uneasy feeling he had something there.

Questions on Meaning

1. Asimov mentions both intelligence and intelligence tests, and he seems to imply that what people generally call "intelligence" is just the ability to score well on a certain kind of test. How do you respond to his statement that such tests could also be created by a carpenter or a farmer?
2. What is the difference, according to most people's thinking, between intelligence and manual dexterity? What does Asimov here imply about such a distinction?
3. Is it important to distinguish between intelligence (ability) and knowledge (learned)? Why or why not?

Questions on Rhetorical Strategy and Style

1. The repairman gives an example of what he means by "smart." See if you can find a concrete example Asimov gives of "intelligence," and comment on the significance of your finding for the success of the essay.
2. When Asimov misses the repairman's joke and gives the wrong answer, the repairman says, apparently only half-jokingly, that Asimov isn't very smart. What is the implied difference between being intelligent and being smart? Is Asimov truly saying that he isn't smart, or how else do you explain the ending line?

Writing Assignments

1. Asimov would seem to argue that there is not an absolute quality or set of abilities we can call intelligence. Do you agree with Asimov about this? Write an essay in which you define what you mean by intelligence.
2. In this essay Asimov uses the rhetorical strategy of definition to discuss intelligence. Write an essay in which you use the strategy of definition to discuss a similar abstract trait of your own choice.

ADVOCATING FOR AN EDUCATION

Kaitlin McCue

O n my first day of high school in a new community, I walked into my first hour classroom full of unfamiliar faces. The students in my history class already knew one another from the many years in which they had attended the same school. I sat and waited for the class to begin. The teacher did the typical introductions and passed out the syllabus. He then gave us the class an assignment to read a chapter in our text and answer questions. Like all the other students, I opened my book and began to read. I realized that I would not be able to understand or complete this assignment in class if I had to read it myself. I got up from my seat and went to talk to the teacher at his desk. I explained to the teacher that I was new to the school and that I had dyslexia, which meant that I would need some help reading this assignment. It took many years to become comfortable with the self-advocacy that I exhibited that day. My experiences in the education system taught me to advocate for myself in order not to get lost in the system and instead to receive a decent education.

Becoming an advocate for myself is something that I had to do to ensure my success. For example, one day I walked into my seventh grade honors science class. While walking to my seat, I noticed that a substitute was sitting in my teacher's seat. The class was excited and began to break away from the everyday class rules. When the teacher got the class in order, we were instructed to read an article in a science

Kaitlin McCue an aspiring photographer from DeWitt, Michigan who is transferring to a four-year school to study photography. She wrote this essay for her WRIT 117 class in Fall 2007.

magazine. The substitute teacher decided that we would go around the room with each student reading a paragraph. As my turn was getting closer and closer, I became more and more nervous. When it was my turn, I looked up and said "pass". The teacher did not respond kindly and said, "you can read, so read." Of course, I really couldn't read, so I packed my books and went to my reading teacher to finish the assignment. My ability to communicate to teachers what I didn't understand and what I needed in order to be able to learn successfully was the key to my success. Without this communication my grades would have suffered and I may have given up on education.

Self-advocacy didn't come naturally to me; it took time, courage and self-motivation. After coming home without understanding the homework assignments I would have to ask my parents and their response was "Why didn't you ask your teacher?" This taught me that I needed to be in charge of what I learned and to get over the fear of people thinking that I didn't understand. Learning this lesson taught me that I am the only person that I can rely on. This allowed me to advocate for myself in any situation, because there is no one else who cares if I don't understand what a fragment is, or who will tell someone to help me. As my own advocate, these are all things that I have learned to do for myself. When I found the courage to tell my peers and teachers about my learning style, I was able to learn with less anxiety.

Unfortunately, our education system allows those who don't advocate for themselves to fail. Many students don't have people who care about there personal success. Without this support they often give up and fail. Some people can't figure out how they learn best, which means they can't communicate what they need to be successful. Others can't find the motivation to learn because they doubt their abilities. As students, we should feel comfortable to go to teachers and explain to them our challenges and insecurities. Without doing this there may be no way for teachers to understand that we are struggling. Many teachers have full classes and may assume that a student isn't putting in the time needed to understand a concept. Despite being outspoken about your challenges you will run into teachers and everyday people that don't understand. This was proven to me when I had a teacher that told me that I would never make it to college, because I am dyslexic. Advocating is used in these situations as well. We have to be strong enough and believe in ourselves more than the people that doubt us. Unfortunately people who aren't willing to believe in us will appear everywhere in life, but we will still have to explain to them our challenges in learning. I have had to tell every teacher, employer, and friend that I am dyslexic. This statement quickly follows typical questions like "do you really see letters backwards" and then a conversation of what it is really like to be dyslexic. These conversations get repetitive and annoying, but they are important to ensure that you and your teacher understand one another. Without students advocating for themselves, even the teachers who are willing to help students overcome insecurities and obstacles don't know how to do so.

5   Perhaps the system itself is trying to educate us on how to become educated. I used to believe that my difficulties with the system stopped me from being successful. Now I believe that my struggles with the system taught me a valuable lesson, which is to be a self-advocate. Because I was prepared for every class and because I educated myself about my rights, I was able to get the support that I needed. The educational system can't spoon-feed us to success. We have to become aware of our own individual learning styles, so that when we leave the classroom we can continue our learning process. No one can make us learn. We have to work hard and be the driving force behind our own education.

COMING TO AN AWARENESS OF LANGUAGE

Malcolm X

On February 21, 1965, Malcolm X, the Black Muslim leader, was shot to death as he addressed an afternoon rally in Harlem. He was thirty-nine years old. In the course of his brief life he had risen from the world of thieving, pimping, and drug pushing to become one of the most articulate and powerful blacks in America during the early 1960s.

With the assistance of Alex Haley, later the author of Roots. *Malcolm X told his story in* The Autobiography of Malcolm X, *a moving account of his search for fulfillment. In the following selection taken from the* Autobiography, *Malcolm X narrates his discovery while in prison of the power of language.*

I've never been one for inaction. Everything I've ever felt strongly about. I've done something about. I guess that's why, unable to do anything else, I soon began writing to people I had known in the hustling world, such as Sammy the Pimp, John Hughes, the gambling house owner, the thief Jumpsteady, and several dope peddlers. I wrote them all about Allah and Islam and Mr. Elijah Muhammad. I had no idea where most of them lived. I addressed their letters in care of the Harlem or Roxbury bars and clubs where I'd known them.

I never got a single reply. The average hustler and criminal was too uneducated to write a letter. I have known many slick, sharp-looking hustlers, who would have you think they had an interest in

---

Reprinted from *The Autobiography of Malcolm X* (1965), CMG Worldwide.

Wall Street; privately, they would get someone else to read a letter if they received one. Besides, neither would I have replied to anyone writing me something as wild as "the white man is the devil."

What certainly went on the Harlem and Roxbury wires was that Detroit Red was going crazy in stir, or else he was trying some hype to shake up the warden's office.

During the years that I stayed in the Norfolk Prison Colony, never did any official directly say anything to me about those letters, although, of course, they all passed through the prison censorship. I'm sure, however, they monitored what I wrote to add to the files which every state and federal prison keeps on the conversion of Negro inmates by the teachings of Mr. Elijah Muhammad.

5   But at that time, I felt that the real reason was that the white man   5
knew that he was the devil.

Later on, I even wrote to the Mayor of Boston, to the Governor of Massachusetts, and to Harry S. Truman. They never answered; they probably never even saw my letters. I handscratched to them how the white man's society was responsible for the black man's condition in this wilderness of North America.

It was because of my letters that I happened to stumble upon starting to acquire some kind of a homemade education.

I became increasingly frustrated at not being able to express what I wanted to convey in letters that I wrote, especially those to Mr. Elijah Muhammad. In the street, I had been the most articulate hustler out there—I had commanded attention when I said something. But now, trying to write simple English, I not only wasn't articulate, I wasn't even functional. How would I sound writing in slang, the way I would *say* it, something such as, "Look, daddy, let me pull your coat about a cat. Elijah Muhammad—"

Many who today hear me somewhere in person, or on television, or those who read something I've said, will think I went to school far beyond the eighth grade. This impression is due entirely to my prison studies.

10   It had really begun back in the Charlestown Prison, when Bimbi   10
first made me feel envy of his stock of knowledge. Bimbi had always taken charge of any conversation he was in, and I had tried to emulate him. But every book I picked up had few sentences which didn't contain anywhere from one to nearly all of the words that might as well have been in Chinese. When I just skipped those words, of

course, I really ended up with little idea of what the book said. So I had come to the Norfolk Prison Colony still going through only book-reading motions. Pretty soon, I would have quit even these motions, unless I had received the motivation that I did.

I saw that the best thing I could do was get hold of a dictionary—to study, to learn some words. I was lucky enough to reason also that I should try to improve my penmanship. It was sad. I couldn't even write in a straight line. It was both ideas together that moved me to request a dictionary along with some tablets and pencils from the Norfolk Prison Colony school.

I spent two days just riffling uncertainly through the dictionary's pages. I'd never realized so many words existed! I didn't know *which* words I needed to learn. Finally, just to start some kind of action, I began copying.

In my slow, painstaking, ragged handwriting, I copied into my tablet everything printed on that first page, down to the punctuation marks.

I believe it took me a day. Then, aloud, I read back, to myself, everything I'd written on the tablet. Over and over, aloud, to myself, I read my own handwriting.

15   I woke up the next morning, thinking about those words—   15
immensely proud to realize that not only had I written so much at one time, but I'd written words that I never knew were in the world. Moreover, with a little effort, I also could remember what many of these words meant. I reviewed the words whose meanings I didn't remember. Funny thing, from the dictionary first page right now, that "aardvark" springs to my mind. The dictionary had a picture of it, a long-tailed, long-eared, burrowing African mammal, which lives off termites caught by sticking out its tongue as an anteater does for ants.

I was so fascinated that I went on—I copied the dictionary's next page. And the same experience came when I studied that. With every succeeding page, I also learned of people and places and events from history. Actually the dictionary is like a miniature encyclopedia. Finally the dictionary's A section had filled a whole tablet—and I went on into the B's. That was the way I started copying what eventually became the entire dictionary. It went a lot faster after so much practice helped me to pick up handwriting speed. Between what I wrote in my tablet, and writing letters, during the rest of my time in prison I would guess I wrote a million words.

I suppose it was inevitable that as my word-base broadened, I could for the first time pick up a book and read and now begin to understand what the book was saying. Anyone who has read a great deal can imagine the new world that opened. Let me tell you something: from then until I left that prison, in every free moment I had, if I was not reading in the library, I was reading on my bunk. You couldn't have gotten me out of books with a wedge. Between Mr. Muhammad's teachings, my correspondence, my visitors . . . and my reading of books, months passed without my even thinking about being imprisoned. In fact, up to then, I never had been so truly free in my life.

POLITICS AND SOCIETY

Everything Isn't Racial Profiling

Linda Chavez

Linda Chavez was born in Albuquerque, New Mexico. She graduated from the University of Colorado and completed further studies at UCLA and the University of Maryland. Chavez is politically conservative on issues such as affirmative action and bilingual education, which has put her in opposition to many in the Hispanic community. In 1985 she became director of the White House Office of Public Liaison for the Reagan Administration and later the chair of the National Commission on Migrant Education under the first Bush Administration. In 1987, after a failed run for the U.S. Senate from Maryland, Chavez served as president of U.S. English, a lobbying organization supporting English as the official language of the United States. In 2001 she was nominated by President Bush to serve as Secretary of Labor, but she withdrew herself due to controversy over the harboring of an illegal immigrant. She is the author of Out of the Barrio: Toward a New Politics of Hispanic Assimilation *(1991);* An Unlikely Conservative: The Transformation of an Ex-Liberal *(2002); and* Betrayal: How Union Bosses Shake Down Their Members and Corrupt American Politics *(2004). Chavez is the founder of the Center for Equal Opportunity. From 1992 to 1996, she was a consultant for the United Nations Subcommittee on Human Rights. Currently she is a Fox News political commentator.*

In this 2002 editorial, she suggests that some aspects of racial profiling may be necessary for the sake of security.

1   **R**acial profiling is an ugly business—and I have been on record   1
opposing it for years. But I'm not opposed to allowing—no,
requiring—airlines to pay closer attention to passengers who fit
a terrorist profile, which includes national origin. The problem is distinguishing between what is permissible, indeed prudent, behavior and
what is merely bigotry. As the Christmas day incident involving an
Arab American Secret Service agent who was denied passage on American Airlines makes clear, it's not always easy to tell the difference.

Racial profiling entails picking someone out for special scrutiny
simply because of his race. It happens when highway patrolmen pull
over blacks who've committed no traffic violations for spot checks but
ignore other drivers who share similar characteristics, say, out-of-state
plates or expensive cars. It happens when security guards at a mall tail
black customers in stores or insist on inspecting only their bags,
ignoring whites. The underlying presumption in these cases is that
blacks are more likely to be involved in criminal acts because of the
color of their skin.

This kind of racial profiling is both morally wrong and ineffec-
tive. But there are times when it makes sense to include race or
national origin in a larger criminal profile, particularly if you're dealing with a crime that has already been committed or is ongoing and
the participants all come from a single ethnic or racial group.

It would make no sense if witnesses identified a six-foot-tall,
blond male fleeing a homicide but police stopped females, short men,
or blacks or Latinos for questioning. Likewise, if you stopped every
tall, blond man, a lot of innocent people would be inconvenienced, if
only temporarily. Which brings us to the case of the Arab American
Secret Service agent.

5   Walid Shater was allowed initially to board an American Airlines   5
plane in Baltimore headed for Texas, carrying a loaded gun, but then
was pulled off the plane, along with a handful of other passengers, for
questioning. In the intervening ninety minutes, Shater's lawyers allege
that he was mistreated and denied the right to fly because he was an
Arab American, while the pilot claims that the agent became loud and
abusive, leading him to keep Shater off the flight.

I can fully sympathize with the agent's anger—but I don't think
the airline acted improperly. I've had encounters similar to Shater's,
largely because of my appearance. When I used to travel frequently in
Europe from the mid-'80s to the mid-'90s, I was routinely questioned

more than other passengers, I suspect because I look vaguely Middle Eastern—or as one airline agent put it, "Your passport's American, but you don't look American."

On a trip from Israel in 1985, where I was an official government guest of the Israelis, security agents at Tel Aviv Airport questioned me for almost an hour. "But you can't keep me from leaving Israel," I protested. "No, but we can keep you from doing so on an airplane," the guard responded. They finally let me go when another passenger, who recognized me from the newspapers, vouched for me.

On another flight, this time from Switzerland, I was asked to deboard the plane after the passengers were in their seats and was questioned about items in my checked luggage. It was humiliating to be called off the plane and to have the passengers told the flight would be delayed because of concerns about one of the passenger's bags.

But I didn't rush to file a discrimination complaint. I didn't like being singled out, but I understood why I was being subjected to more scrutiny. At the time I was hassled, Middle Eastern terrorism was very prevalent in Europe, and female terrorists were operating as well as men, usually on stolen or phony passports. It wasn't unreasonable for airlines to look at me a little more closely than other passengers given these facts.

In Shater's case, nineteen Arab terrorists killed more than three thousand Americans on September 11, and several of the hijackers possessed stolen identification cards and pilots' uniforms. It wasn't unreasonable for the American Airlines pilot to be extra cautious with Shater under the circumstances, despite his official ID. As a law enforcement officer himself, Shater might have cut these guys a little more slack.

Sure it's unpleasant to be a suspect when you're innocent. But it's worse to overlook terrorists because we ignored their pertinent characteristics. I sometimes felt annoyed when I was singled out, but I also felt safer because the airlines were doing their job.

Questions on Meaning

1. The author distinguishes between profiling that is "permissible, indeed prudent, behavior and what is merely bigotry." What are the differences?
2. What does the case of Walid Shater represent? Why were the authorities justified in detaining him, in the author's opinion? Do you agree?
3. Were you surprised that Chavez, as a Hispanic and having been profiled herself, would argue in favor of it? Explain how someone might be able to hold a position on a matter that has disadvantaged Hispanics and other people of color.

Questions on Rhetorical Strategy and Style

1. Notice that the author asserts from the outset her feelings about racial profiling. Why is this important?
2. In the editorial the author recounts incidents in which she was profiled. What is the purpose of recounting these experiences? Even though they were humiliating for her, what tone does she use to detail those incidences? Why?
3. What is the ultimate purpose of the editorial? How does it attempt to educate readers on the issues of civil rights and national security?

Writing Assignments

1. Racial profiling is a particularly contentious issue in this post-9/11 world. Conduct research on the matter and write an essay explaining a few of the perspectives that make it so polarized.
2. Write an essay attempting to convey the effects of racial profiling on individuals. Base your essay on public accounts of profiling or on first- or secondhand experiences.

❧ WE BOTH HAVE OUR SCARS ❧

Anthony Lee Sands

*Dedicated to the 1-182 C Battery Veterans, and the 1-182
A Battery Deployment. We pray that we all return home
safely and continue and fulfill our dreams in life.*

I began to feel the blood drying on my hand even though it had only been a few seconds since I placed the bandage on the side of my friend's face. With his arm around my neck and me grasping him tightly, we began a slow walk down to the ground floor with gunshots ringing in the street. It turned to silence for a moment before the distinct sound of a SAW (squad automatic weapon) could be heard firing a hundred some rounds. It was like a lion roaring in a jungle to let everyone know who was king.

We reached the ground floor after several minutes of working our way down the narrow, dust-filled stairs. Fatigue from the harsh conditions and the physical punishment our bodies had been taking over the course of the last seven weeks overwhelmed us. Our feet gripped the shell casings on the hard dirt floor as we began working our way though the series of rooms and hallways to get outside. Dust remained in the air of the buildings like fog on country roads. My buddy's head was now almost resting on my shoulder, which allowed the blood from the side of his face to slowly drip on my BDUs (battle dress uniform).

Before I even took that step outside, I had already taken a deep breath of the dust-filled air—which seemed to be gold dust because sunlight penetrated the dark room—to call for help. I heard a reply telling me to wait where I was, but we needed to find shade. We were

---

Anthony Lee Sands is currently serving in the US Army National Guard. He wrote this essay in his WRIT 117 class, knowing he would be deployed to Iraq before he could prepare his portfolio and finish the course.

in a 115 degree heat, wearing body armor that was too small and now made me feel as if it wanted to crush my ribs and lungs rather than protect them from bullets. My helmet felt as if it weighed fifty pounds, and it had been taking a toll on my neck as I'd been wearing it the last seven weeks. I was also carrying 250 rounds on my LBV (load bearing vest) and Angel, my M16A2 rifle, which I had named after my now ex-girlfriend. Because of the black metal, heat, and firing rounds, I could have cooked eggs and bacon on my rifle. As we walked to the other side of the building for shade, we both began to drink a full canteen of water. We sat waiting for help to arrive.

The gunfire turned to silence not too long after we had taken our seats in the shade. The war game had long since been over for us. After a few minutes of silence, I turned to my friend and apologized. He pulled his arm back and as I looked into his one uncovered eye, I knew what was coming. He punched me so hard it made me fall over even though we were seated. As I got myself upright and held the side of my face, he said, "We're even. And I got you covered." We then began to laugh.

When a soldier tells you, "I got you covered," he is telling you one of two things: "I am going give you suppressing fire while you do what you got to do," or "I'm going to make sure you don't get in trouble." The only time someone has ever told me "I got you covered" to help get me out of trouble was back at basic training in Fort Sill, Oklahoma. I had become friends with a man flying down to Ft. Sill. We both were in the split option for the National Guard, meaning we were going to basic between our junior and senior years of high school. I had just turned 18 the day we got on the airplane. We both went to reception together at 95th, where they process you so you can go to basic training. Then we both ended up in the same basic training battery. By the start of basic training, I knew the name of his girlfriend and sister, the stories of his childhood and how much he loved and missed his parents.

However, we were in different platoons, which meant we were only able to talk on rare occasions. On our final field training exercise, I was able to share a fighting position with him. We lived and slept next to each other for a full week. It was hell living out there in the jungle, but there was no better man I could have picked to cover me out there.

During the field exercise, the battery went to Liberty City, a town that was built like a village over in Iraq. I would not be making the assault on the town because I was selected to be a terrorist. I found myself on the 2nd floor of some building. It seemed so real; it looked as if someone actually lived in that building. It was a place I would only have lived in if I was homeless.

A squad approached my building and, since I was two stories up, I could see them as clear as day. I fired several rounds and the instructor outside made seven out of the eight soldiers lay on the ground showing that they had died. However, one was able to get into the building. I repositioned myself in a room that led to the stairway. I listened for the sound of his feet coming up the stairway. I could no longer hear gunfire outside because all I heard was the sound of my pounding heart and the slow, deep and long breaths I was taking to calm myself down. I heard the soldier come up the stairs, and wonder if he could hear the sound of my breath and heartbeat, I stepped into the doorway with my weapon pointed in the direction of the staircase. To my surprise, I was looking into the eyes of another man and like an innocent child with his father's gun I pulled my trigger. I never heard the round go off, but I saw him drop to the ground as if I had really killed him.

A hundred thoughts went though my mind in a heartbeat. My weapon had been on his cheek when I fired my blank round. The blank adaptor guard at the tip of every training soldier's weapon redirects the pressure, so when you fire a blank round it does not injure the man in front of you. When I had fired that round, the pressure from the shot redirected straight into the soldiers face. It was only a moment later when I went to pull out a bandage to put on his face that I noticed the soldier I had shot was my good friend.

When he got back from the hospital, people asked him what happened to his face. He always started out the same way. "This bastard named Sands shot me in the face." He would always take a moment to pause and laugh about it.

My friend has a scar right under his left eye and I have a bad memory of shooting a friend in the face. It has always been something I have wanted to forget. I saw him once nearly a year later. We talked about several things, but for nearly a half hour we joked and laughed about the time I shot him.

We would all laugh, not because it's funny or some kind of joke, but because soldiers don't always have a lot to laugh about. Laughing takes our minds off what really does happen to us.

A Brother's Murder

Brent Staples

Brent Staples (1951–) was born in Chester, Penn., a factory town south of Philadelphia. He received a PhD in Psychology from the University of Chicago. He is a journalist whose first full-time job was staff reporter with the Chicago Sun-Times *in 1983–85. In 1987 he became editor of the* New York Times Book Review *and is also assistant metropolitan editor. Staples was given the Annisfield Wolff Award for his memoir:* Parallel Time: Growing up in Black and White *(1995).*

1   It has been more than two years since my telephone rang with the news that my younger brother Blake—just 22 years old—had been murdered. The young man who killed him was only 24. Wearing a ski mask, he emerged from a car, fired six times at close range with a massive .44 Magnum, then fled. The two had once been inseparable friends. A senseless rivalry—beginning, I think, with an argument over a girlfriend—escalated from posturing, to threats, to violence, to murder. The way the two were living, death could have come to either of them from anywhere. In fact, the assailant had already survived multiple gunshot wounds from an incident much like the one in which my brother lost his life.

As I wept for Blake, I felt wrenched backward into events and circumstances that had seemed light-years gone. Though a decade apart, we both were raised in Chester, Pennsylvania, an angry, heavily black, heavily poor, industrial city southwest of Philadelphia. There, in the 1960s, I was introduced to mortality, not by the old and failing, but by beautiful young men who lay wrecked after sudden explosions of violence. The first, I remember from my 14th year—Johnny, brash lover of fast cars, stabbed to death two doors from my house in a fight over a pool game. The next year, my teen-age cousin, Wesley, whom I loved very much, was shot dead. The summers blur. Milton, an angry young neighbor, shot a crosstown rival, wounding him badly. William, another teen-age neighbor, took a shotgun blast to the shoulder in some urban drama and displayed his bandages proudly. His brother, Leonard, severely beaten, lost an eye and donned a black patch. It went on.

I recall not long before I left for college, two local Vietnam veterans—one from the Marines, one from the Army—arguing fiercely, nearly at blows about which outfit had done the most in the war. The most killing, they meant. Not much later, I read in a magazine article that set that dispute in a context. In the story, a noncommissioned officer—a sergeant, I believe—said he would pass up any number of affluent, suburban-born recruits to get hard-core soldiers from the inner city. They jumped into the rice paddies with "their manhood on their sleeves," I believe he said. These two items—the veterans arguing and the sergeant's words—still characterize for me the circumstances under which black men in their teens and 20's kill one another with such frequency. With a touchy paranoia born of living battered lives, they are desperate to be *real* men. Killing is only *machismo* taken to the extreme. Incursions to be punished by death were many and minor, and they remain so: they include stepping on the wrong toe, literally; cheating in a drug deal; simply saying "I dare you" to someone holding a gun; crossing territorial lines in a gang dispute. My brother grew up to wear his manhood on his sleeve. And when he died, he was in that group—black, male, and in its teens and early 20's—that is far and away the most likely to murder or be murdered.

I left the East Coast after college, spent the mid- and late-1970's in Chicago as a graduate student, taught for a time, then became a journalist. Within 10 years of leaving my hometown, I was overeducated and "upwardly mobile," ensconced on a quiet, tree-lined street where voices raised in anger were scarcely ever heard. The telephone, like some grim umbilical cord, kept me connected to the old world with news of deaths, imprisonings, and misfortune. I felt emotionally beaten up. Perhaps to protect my self, I added a psychological dimension to the physical distance I had already achieved. I rarely visited my hometown. I shut it out.

5   As I fled the past, so Blake embraced it. On Christmas of 1983, I   5
traveled from Chicago to a black section of Roanoke, Virginia, where
he then lived. The desolate public housing projects, the hopeless, idle
young men crashing against one another—these reminded me of the
embittered town we'd grown up in. It was a place where once I would
have been comfortable, or at least sure of myself. Now, hearing of my
brother's foray into crime, his scrapes with police and street thugs, I
was scared, unsteady on foreign terrain.

I saw Blake's romance with the street life, and the hustler image
had flowered dangerously. One evening that late December, standing
in some Roanoke dive among drug dealers and grim, hair-trigger
losers, I told him I feared for his life. He had affected the image of the
tough he wanted to be. But behind the dark glasses and the swagger, I
glimpsed the baby-faced toddler I'd once watched over. I nearly wept.
I wanted desperately for him to live. The young think themselves
immortal, and a dangerous light shone in his eyes as he spoke laugh-
ingly of making fools of the policemen who had raided his apartment
looking for drugs. He cried out as I took his right hand. A line of
stitches lay between the thumb and index finger. Kickback from a
shotgun, he explained, nothing serious. Gunplay had become part of
his life.

I lacked the language simply to say: Thousands have lived this for
you and died. I fought the urge to lift him bodily and shake him. This
place and the way you are living smells of death to me, I said. Take
some time away, I said. Let's go downtown tomorrow and buy a plane
ticket anywhere, take a bus trip, anything to get away and cool things
off. He took my alarm casually. We arranged to meet the following
night—an appointment he would not keep. We embraced as though
through glass. I drove away.

As I stood in my apartment in Chicago holding the receiver that
evening in February 1984, I felt as though part of my soul had been
cut away. I questioned myself then, and I still do. Did I not reach
back soon or earnestly enough for him? For weeks I awoke crying
from a recurrent dream in which I chased him, urgently trying to get
him to read a document I had, as though reading it would protect
him from what had happened in waking life. His eyes shining like
black diamonds, he smiled and danced just out of my grasp. When I
reached for him, I caught only the space where he had been.

Questions on Meaning

1. This essay asks poignantly, "Am I my brother's keeper?" Staples describes his efforts to save his younger brother from the streets but doubts his own effectiveness. Do you think that he did enough? What else could he have done?
2. Staples escaped the streets through college and writing, escaping to a quiet street where no one raises their voice. What happens to people like Staples who leave their past behind? What have they lost?
3. Romance defines the street life, boys trying to prove that they are tough, that they are men. Staples talks of the toughness of street kids in Viet Nam. Why do boys try so hard to be tough? What does it do for them? What does it cost them?

Questions on Rhetorical Strategy and Style

1. This essay is personal and close. The reader is brought into Staples's own intense personal experiences and into his self-doubt. How does this closeness affect you as reader?
2. Nearly every other sentence in the essay begins with "I" so that the reader is right there with the narrator on this trip into memory. Why is the first person so effective in this essay?
3. The ending of the essay makes clear that Staples has forgiven himself for not saving his brother. Why does this image of the boy dancing away from him show that Staples is both sad and resigned?

Writing Assignments

1. If possible, find Viet Nam or Gulf War veterans and ask them about their experiences. How old were they? Why did they go? What did they learn? Write about your interviews, showing what you have learned about young men and women coming of age.
2. Recall an experience with one of your brothers or sisters, or with a friend or relative. Describe the experience so that the reader can understand what the experience meant to you at the time and what it means to you now.

3. How much freedom do we have in life? Are our choices determined by where we grow up and by the people we know? Write about this freedom or lack thereof using examples from your own life and from the lives of those you have known.

Request for a Declaration of War

Franklin Delano Roosevelt

Franklin Delano Roosevelt (1882–1945) was born in Hyde Park, New York, to a powerful, wealthy family. Roosevelt entered politics after graduating from Harvard University and Columbia Law School. Having served New York as state senator and later as governor, Roosevelt successfully ran for president in 1932. As part of his campaign, he promised to move the country out of the depression that had gripped it since the stock-market crash of 1929. With his wife, Eleanor, President Roosevelt enacted programs and policies to help the unemployed workers and get the country "back on its feet".

When World War II hit Europe in 1939, Roosevelt pledged to assist France and England in their battle against the onslaught of Nazi Germany. And when the Japanese bombed Pearl Harbor on December 7, 1941, he committed the United States to the global war. Having survived crippling polio as a young man, Roosevelt suffered from declining health during the latter years of the war. He died in April 1945, just months before the Allied victories in Europe and Asia. In this address to the U.S. Congress, Roosevelt calls on the nation to marshal its resources to fight an enemy half a world away.

Message to Congress, December 8, 1941
Franklin D. Roosevelt
Request for a Declaration of War

Message to Congress

1   Yesterday, December 7, 1941—a date which will live in infamy—   1
the United States of America was suddenly and deliberately
attacked by naval and air forces of the Empire of Japan.

The United States was at peace with that nation, and, at the
solicitation of Japan, was still in conversation with its government and
its emperor looking toward the maintenance of peace in the Pacific.
Indeed, one hour after Japanese air squadrons had commenced
bombing in Oahu, the Japanese ambassador to the United States and
his colleague delivered to the secretary of state a formal reply to a
recent American message. While this reply stated that it seemed
useless to continue the existing diplomatic negotiations, it contained
no threat or hint of war or armed attack.

It will be recorded that the distance of Hawaii from Japan makes
it obvious that the attack was deliberately planned many days or even
weeks ago. During the intervening time the Japanese government has
deliberately sought to deceive the United States by false statements
and expressions of hope for continued peace.

The attack yesterday on the Hawaiian Islands has caused severe
damage to American naval and military forces. Very many American
lives have been lost. In addition, American ships have been reported
torpedoed on the high seas between San Francisco and Honolulu.

5   Yesterday the Japanese government also launched an attack   5
against Malaya.

Last night Japanese forces attacked Hong Kong.

Last night Japanese forces attacked Guam.

Last night Japanese forces attacked the Philippine Islands.

Last night the Japanese attacked Wake Island.

10   This morning the Japanese attacked Midway Island.   10

Japan has, therefore, undertaken a surprise offensive extending
throughout the Pacific area. The facts of yesterday speak for
themselves. The people of the United States have already formed their

opinions and well understand the implications to the very life and safety of our nation.

As commander in chief of the Army and Navy I have directed that all measures be taken for our defense.

Always will we remember the character of the onslaught against us. No matter how long it may take us to overcome this premeditated invasion, the American people, in their righteous might, will win through to absolute victory. I believe I interpret the will of the Congress and of the people when I assert that we will not only defend ourselves to the uttermost but will make very certain that this form of treachery shall never endanger us again.

Hostilities exist. There is no blinking at the fact that our people, our territory, and our interests are in grave danger.

15 With confidence in our armed forces—with the unbounded 15 determination of our people—we will gain the inevitable triumph— so help us God.

I ask that the Congress declare that since the unprovoked and dastardly attack by Japan on Sunday, December 7, a state of war has existed between the United States and the Japanese Empire.

Questions on Meaning

1. How did President Roosevelt characterize Japan's actions? Why did it matter that the attack on Pearl Harbor had been planned weeks before?
2. How would you assess Roosevelt's confidence in the will of the American people to fight? On what do you base your assessment?

Questions on Rhetorical Strategy and Style

1. How did Roosevelt's first paragraph—particularly the expression "a date which will live in infamy"—set the tone for his appeal? How did this introduction work on both a rational and an emotional level?
2. Describe the effect of the refrain "Last night Japanese forces" as Roosevelt cited examples of recent military actions undertaken by the Japanese. How would Roosevelt's appeal have been affected if he had simply summarized these attacks in paragraph form?
3. According to Roosevelt, the Japanese actions were causes, and the only possible effect was a declaration of war. Explain how the president brought his audience to this conclusion.

Writing Assignments

1. Write a paper analyzing the effectiveness of Roosevelt's language in this speech. Focus on rhetorical features such as word choice, images, and sentence structure and rhythm.
2. Read several historical accounts of the period immediately preceding the attack on Pearl Harbor. Write a paper exploring the mood of the American people with regard to war, the pressures on the government to enter the war, and the impact of the attack on consolidating public opinion.

FAMILY AND COMMUNITY

The Company Man

Ellen Goodman

*Ellen Goodman (1941–), was born in Newton, Massa-
chusetts. A graduate of Radcliffe College (1963), Goodman
worked for* Newsweek *and* The Detroit Free Press *before
joining* The Boston Globe *in 1967. In addition to writing a regular column for the* Globe, "At Large," *which has
been syndicated since 1976, Goodman also is a frequent
radio and television commentator. The recipient of a
Pulitzer Prize for distinguished commentary in 1980,
Goodman has published a number of collections of her
columns—including* Close to Home *(1979) and* At Large
*(1981)—as well as an interview-based review of the impact
of the feminist movement—* Making Sense *(1989). Goodman's essays, which often probe very personal aspects of late
20th century America, are generally a blend of irony and
satire. Note how Goodman uses her skills of observation and
description to quickly dispatch the workaholic company
man in this classic Goodman-style essay.*

1   He worked himself to death, finally and precisely, at 3:00 A.M.   1
Sunday morning.
The obituary didn't say that, of course. It said that he died
of a coronary thrombosis—I think that was it—but everyone among
his friends and acquaintances knew it instantly. He was a perfect Type
A, a workaholic, a classic, they said to each other and shook their
heads—and thought for five or ten minutes about the way they lived.

This man who worked himself to death finally and precisely at
3:00 A.M. Sunday morning—on his day off—was fifty-one years old
and a vice-president. He was, however, one of six vice-presidents, and

one of three who might conceivably—if the president died or retired soon enough—have moved to the top spot. Phil knew that.

He worked six days a week, five of them until eight or nine at night, during a time when his own company had begun the four-day week for everyone but the executives. He worked like the Important People. He had no outside "extracurricular interests," unless, of course, you think about a monthly golf game that way. To Phil, it was work. He always ate egg salad sandwiches at his desk. He was, of course, overweight, by 20 or 25 pounds. He thought it was okay, though, because he didn't smoke.

5   On Saturdays, Phil wore a sports jacket to the office instead of a   5
suit, because it was the weekend.

He had a lot of people working for him, maybe sixty, and most of them liked him most of the time. Three of them will be seriously considered for his job. The obituary didn't mention that.

But it did list his "survivors" quite accurately. He is survived by his wife, Helen, forty-eight years old, a good woman of no particular marketable skills, who worked in an office before marrying and mothering. She had, according to her daughter, given up trying to compete with his work years ago, when the children were small. A company friend said, "I know how much you will miss him." And she answered, "I already have."

"Missing him all these years," she must have given up part of herself which had cared too much for the man. She would be "well taken care of."

His "dearly beloved" eldest of the "dearly beloved" children is a hard-working executive in a manufacturing firm down South. In the day and a half before the funeral, he went around the neighborhood researching his father, asking the neighbors what he was like. They were embarrassed.

10   His second child is a girl, who is twenty-four and newly married.   10
She lives near her mother and they are close, but whenever she was alone with her father, in a car driving somewhere, they had nothing to say to each other.

The youngest is twenty, a boy, a high-school graduate who has spent the last couple of years, like a lot of his friends, doing enough odd jobs to stay in grass and food. He was the one who tried to grab at his father, and tried to mean enough to him to keep the man at home. He was his father's favorite. Over the last two years, Phil stayed up nights worrying about the boy.

The boy once said, "My father and I only board here."

At the funeral, the sixty-year-old company president told the forty-eight-year-old widow that the fifty-one-year-old deceased had meant much to the company and would be missed and would be hard to replace. The widow didn't look him in the eye. She was afraid he would read her bitterness and, after all, she would need him to straighten out the finances—the stock options and all that.

Phil was overweight and nervous and worked too hard. If he wasn't at the office, he was worried about it. Phil was a Type A, a heart-attack natural. You could have picked him out in a minute from a lineup.

So when he finally worked himself to death, at precisely 3:00 A.M. Sunday morning, no one was really surprised.

By 5:00 P.M. the afternoon of the funeral, the company president had begun, discreetly of course, with care and taste, to make inquiries about his replacement. One of three men. He asked around: "Who's been working the hardest?"

Questions on Meaning

1. Goodman gives us a few peeks at Phil—the man, the executive, the father. What do you think Phil thought of himself? What do you think Phil would feel about the reactions of his family and his boss to his untimely death?
2. How much time did Phil really work? Divide his day into four categories: work, family, recreation, and socializing. Reread the essay, estimating the time he spent in each activity each week.
3. What drove Phil to work so hard? What was his goal? What does Goodman say about his chance of reaching his goal?

Questions on Rhetorical Strategy and Style

1. What killed Phil: His heart? His lifestyle? His hard-driving boss? Reread the essay and highlight the passages that give clues to the cause of Phil's death. Then glance back at the passages you have marked and identify the cause and effect passages that are related.
2. Describe Goodman's tone. What does it tell us about her feelings for Phil, for his wife, for his children, for his boss, for his company, and for his lifestyle?
3. Show where Goodman uses repetition to underscore a point, such as "at 3 a.m. Sunday," "the obituary didn't say that," and "dearly beloved." Describe the effect on the essay of these repetitious phrases.

Writing Assignments

1. Everyone knows someone who is a classic Type A and lives like Phil. Describe a Type A personality you know, and compare and contrast that person's lifestyle to Phil. What would you tell the person about his or her lifestyle if the person would listen?
2. Clearly Phil was out of touch—with his family, with his neighbors, with himself. Think of someone you have grown out of touch with because you have simply been too busy to spend time with them or to stay in touch. How do you think this person would react if suddenly you were gone, like Phil? Write an essay in which you describe what you imagine this person's feelings would be if something untimely were to happen to you. What do you think this person would comment about your lifestyle?

MODERNIZED MAN

Whitnie Preuss

1 Since the women's lib movement, stereotypical views of women have constantly been revised whereas the stereotypical "norms" for men have remained stagnant. In terms of the home and workplace, women have been given recognition and are considered an equal counterpart in today's society. Women now have the ability to do what was considered a "man's" job, which in turn has given women the capability to provide for themselves and their families financially. However, if a woman is providing for their household the question must be asked, "Who is going to raise the kids if mom works full-time?" It's not typical for society to accept men doing what is still considered a "woman's" job, so when a man decides to be Mr. Mom, misconceptions arise.

In the fifties, *Leave It to Beaver* portrayed the common American household for many, showing a mother who took care of the home and kids while the father went to work. Men were the breadwinners who left before the break of dawn to spend long hours away from their home. This was considered justified because men were men and their only job was to support the family financially. The majority of men weren't supposed to help clean the house or take care of the kids when they came home; after all, they already fulfilled their role by bringing the paycheck in the door.

Times have changed since then and presently there are more women than ever who have joined the work force. A lot of women are being compensated as much or even more than men thanks to the women's movement. However, this has forced families to discuss who should work and who should raise the kids. Parents do have options, such as

---

A Lansing native, Whitnie Preuss is studying to be a medical office administrator. She wrote this essay for her WRIT 117 class in Fall 2007.

family, friends, or a babysitter in order for both of them to work. However, daycare has become an increasing expense that some simply can't afford, and many parents do not wish to have their children raised by someone else. An alternative option that families have decided to embark on is to have the dad stay home and tend to the kids while the mom works full-time in order to bring home the bacon. By choosing so, however, men are subjected to criticism and viewed as failures within their social circle even in the twenty-first century. Still, my husband decided to stay at home after trying all other options, and now we confront scrutiny more often than not.

Because of this choice, people presume that there is another reason beyond why he stays at home to take care of the kids.

"This can't be in the best interest for the family, why doesn't he work? What's wrong with him?" I have heard people say before I even begin to explain our circumstances.

"So, he wants his wife to take care of him. He wants to lounge all day on the couch and watch T.V., or play on the computer while he ignores the kids, huh?" I have heard this garbage from both men and women.

More surprising is when women have accused him of not being a real man for doing the very job that they do. This double standard is coming from the mouths of the same mothers who pleaded that being a stay-at-home mom is the hardest job of all. These particular women do not believe that a man should or even could handle "their" job all day, everyday. How could these women judge men as being inadequate for doing a "woman's" job? Understandably so, there are many duties that a stay-at-home mom must accomplish consistently, and even I must admit, I didn't have faith in my husband's ability to fill my shoes either. However, I have learned a man can contribute to his household everything a woman can, if he is willing.

When my husband and I agreed that he would stay at home with our children so I could further my career he had to adapt quickly. He had to have the ability to do the many jobs I had been doing for years: multi-tasking as a babysitter, housekeeper, cook, receptionist, janitor, counselor, accountant, teacher, referee, scheduling coordinator, coach, disciplinary supervisor, gopher and psychoanalyst. It was definitely stressful at first, but over a short period of time he has proven to me that he is capable of doing such a demanding job with compassion.

Our children are being consistently benefited from the emotional growth they have received because their dad stays at home. The quality time he spends with them far outweighs the financial sacrifice, and now having this extra time, he provides true balance and support for our family. He has a remarkable influence on them by being there for them when pressures arise. Whether its homework or a conflict with a peer his teaching ability with childhood dilemmas is irreproachable. He is able to calmly rationalize situations with them more quickly and be more patient than even I have learned how to do, yet. Our children do not know their father just as an instant lottery ticket or solely as a dictator, but now as their personal provider and confidant—a feeling earned by his time skillfully spent with them.

10 Men should not feel guilty or embarrassed to work from home. 10 Granted they are not receiving money but, hopefully, they are paid with the reward of gratitude from their family. Most importantly, our children now have a better example of gender equality when they see both parents demonstrate equal responsibility to the household.

The misconception that most people have for a man who chooses to be a stay-at-home dad makes it virtually impossible for him to escape the shadow cast by society's opinion. A family must be determined not to be affected by what other members of society think. This is a family's choice to make, one which suits the family's needs, not society's. People must not emasculate a man for taking this role, because being more of a father does not make him less of a man.

⇜ NO TIME FOR SNOWMEN ⇝

Zoltan Krompecher

I have deployed on numerous occasions during my nineteen years in the Army. On every occasion, both as a Special Forces soldier and as an Intelligence officer, I deployed as a member of a unit. During those times, the frenetic pace of preparing a group of soldiers to leave had distracted me from thinking about the actual deployment itself. Now, however, I find myself in the unique position of an individual deploying to a unit already in Iraq. This time I have had months to reflect, and I write this because this deployment has rekindled long forgotten memories. As the war progresses, I hope this piece reaches out to other individuals who might find themselves in similar situations.

"To the world I am an individual. To an individual, I am the world."

SFC James Smith attached that quotation to an email he sent me four years ago. Unfortunately, I never took the message seriously until I recently received orders for a brief deployment to Iraq. Now, as my departure date looms, I find fault regarding the opportunities I missed to spend time with my family during this past winter.

Up here in West Point, N.Y., winter is long and cold. And winter, reflected off the uniforms of cadets and the granite walls of the United States Military Academy, is gray. In fact, cadets often remark that winter here often takes on the appearance of "Castle Greyskull."

Zoltan Krompecher was a teaching intern in the developmental writing program at Lansing Community College. He is currently serving in the US Army Special Forces and wrote this essay for *Operation Homecoming*, a collection of writings by military personnel returning home from the wars in Iraq and Afghanistan.

Reprinted from *CBS News Online*, February 24, 2005, CBS News.

Indeed, my cynical outlook toward winter only changed because of a lesson my daughter Leah taught me.

The leaves have fallen, and winter is on its way.

5   When Leah was two, we went sledding for the first time: Just the two of us—daddy and daughter—out enjoying the Michigan snow. After each ride down the hill, I would tow her back up while she sat on the sled. During one of our treks up, I overheard her crying and looked back to see that one of her snow boots had fallen off at the bottom of the hill. I picked her up, placed her foot in my jacket and headed down the hill to retrieve her boot. Little did I know that she would forever remember that incident as a pleasurable one because it was a moment in which we bonded. Now, any mention of snow and she responds happily with, "Daddy, remember when we went sledding and my boot 'felled' off?" quickly following with, "Daddy, when can we go sledding again?" That was two years ago, and she still remembers it as if it were yesterday.

I look out my window and see the frozen Hudson River covered with ice which resembles cold steel. For some reason, I find myself feeling as cold inside as the chilling wind that slices through everything and forces people to scatter for reprieve.

One night during this past December, I read Leah The Snowy Day before she went to sleep. The next morning revealed 3 inches of fresh powder. "Daddy, can we go outside and play like Peter did in his book?" Leah asked me. I replied that I had to get to work but maybe we could build a snowman after I returned home. Unfortunately, it was so dark by the time I returned from work that there was no time for snowmen.

Every morning, I walk outside to kick the icicles hanging off my jeep before driving to work through the slush-covered roads.

In January, it snowed again, and Leah came running up to me with her pull-on boots on the wrong feet, an unzipped jacket and mittens. There she stood in front of me: smiling eagerly in hopes of playing in the snow. Sadly, my response was not so soothing. Put simply, I felt that I had no time to play with my children. I was preparing to go to war. Eventually, she stopped asking me to play in the snow with her and instead would sit quietly in her reading chair while I called Ft. Bragg. Her silence rang in my ears.

10   *As I walk around the campus, harbingers of spring greet me: islands of grass appear, and I no longer wear my parka to work.*

In March, the sun began melting away both the snow and winter's memories. During one of the unseasonably warm days, I arrived home late but just in time to witness Leah attempting to play kickball with the neighborhood children. In the middle of the field was another father from across the street. He moved towards her and gently rolled the ball as she stood uncertainly at home plate. She responded with a kick and laughed hysterically as she attempted to run the bases in a circuitous fashion. It hit me. As I sat there in my car, I realized how that should be me out on that plate. That should be me guiding my daughter to first base and then deliberately miss tagging her out as she rounded third for a homerun. I quickly understood how I should have taken her sledding to see if perhaps we could make it down a hill without her boot falling off.

The next day, I saw Leah ride her bike by herself. I asked my wife, Tina, who had fastened Leah's bicycle helmet and helped her move the bike from our backyard to the front of the house. Tina responded that Leah had found her helmet in the closet, dragged her bike to the front of the house, and proceeded to ride. This was the first time she did not have anybody walking by her side ensuring that she would not fall: this time she was riding alone. It was then that I grasped that she was growing up and would not always need me.

Now it is spring, and last night, as I was putting her to bed, Leah looked up at me and said, "Daddy, I have tears in my eyes because you will be leaving." With that statement, I resolved to take SFC Smith's quote to heart and decided to "be the world" to my family. Years from now, I do not want to be the guy who sits alone sifting through a box of pictures trying to recapture fading memories because he left his children clinging to unfulfilled promises.

April has arrived, and there is little evidence of the long winter. I have put the sled away until next year. Winter is over, and I am leaving for Iraq. My daughter is growing. Man, I wish it would snow just one more time.

15 *It snowed ten days after CPT Krompecher began this article. He and his girls spent a wonderful afternoon sledding and topped it all off with rounds of hot chocolate. He left for Iraq in May.* 15

Death of a Homeless Man

Scott Russell Sanders

Scott Russell Sanders (1945–) was born in Memphis, Ten-nessee, attended Brown University and took a Ph.D. at Cambridge University. He writes on a variety of subjects for "little" magazines such as The Georgia Review *and* The North American Review *and for more commercial publications such as* Omni *and* Isaac Asimov's Science Fiction Magazine. *His published books include* Wonder's Hidden: Audubon's Early Years *(1984),* Hear the Wind Blow: American Folksongs Retold *(1985), and* The Par-adise of Bombs *(1987). His writing is characteristically rich in detail and focused on the ironies and complexities of human experience. You will find painfully vivid de-scription in the essay that follows.*

This past winter, not long after Christmas, a man named John Griffin burned to death in South Boston. He was fifty-five, a veteran of the Korean War, an alcoholic, well-known and liked by his neighbors, who remembered him as a streetwise philosopher, a genial storyteller, gracious and kindly and full of song. His body, from which all the clothing had been burned away except for tatters at ankles and wrists, was found twenty feet from Dorchester Bay. Evi-dently Griffin had collapsed on his way to the water, for staggery foot-prints marked a trail back over the sand to his plywood hovel. No one knows what set his clothes alight, whether a cigarette or the fire of twigs and cardboard he'd been using to keep warm.

So there you have it, the death of a homeless man. At this point a good journalist would tell you how many hundreds of thousands, even how many millions, of souls go to sleep cold and hungry and

Published in *The Progressive*, March 1987.

roofless each night in this rich land. Although I am thankful for those conscientious reporters, I am not any sort of journalist, good or bad; I am a novelist, snagged on particulars. I cannot get beyond that charred body of John Griffin, those wristlets and anklets of cloth, those eloquent footprints in the sand, the quenching waters only a few paces beyond his outstretched arms. Instead of brooding on statistics about poverty, I keep seeing his little shanty cobbled together out of scavenged plywood, the cigarette butts and empty vodka bottles strewn on the ground.

As it happens, one of those who passed by John Griffin's homestead almost daily (while jogging) was Boston Mayor Raymond Flynn. Another who saw him regularly was a minister, Leonard Coopenwrath. Both men described Griffin as a friend, and both attended his funeral, along with a cardinal, the police commissioner, the state secretary for human affairs, and other dignitaries. No one could figure out what to do with Griffin alive, but they turned out in force to bury him.

Mayor Flynn was quoted in the papers as saying, "It goes to show you that this country is not meeting the needs of people with physical and mental problems." Indeed, indeed. The mayor seems to be a compassionate man, and so I respect his grief as genuine, although it occurs to me that the city of Boston, as the local portion of "this country," ought to shoulder part of the blame for Griffin's suffering.

As if in counterpoint, the Reverend Coopenwrath observed, "I don't think the system failed him. He wanted to live basically apart from shelters and we must respect that." I'm all for respecting a man's desires, but if those include a preference for spending the Boston winter in a plywood lean-to instead of a public shelter, I think I would take a hard look at the shelter. I would ask what sort of help this Korean War veteran received for his alcoholism, where he last worked, what agency last trained him for a job, what doctors last examined him; what relatives or neighbors or church ever thought of taking him in.

When I reflect on what my nation is up to, what it is achieving with all its huffing and puffing, I do not think about the Gross National Product or the Dow Jones Industrial Average; I think about John Griffin. The GNP, as everyone knows, or should know, is gross indeed, including the price of Griffin's funeral and vodka while ignoring the value of his stories and songs. The stock market see-saws wildly at news of a polyp on the President's colon, but does not so much as tremble over the incineration of John Griffin, would not tremble even if the suffering of all the jobless, homeless, futureless people in America could be added together by some calculus into a Gross Misery Product.

There is no such calculus, for the simple reason that suffering, like death, is personal. Each of us meets it, or avoids it, inside the arena of his or her own skin. You can tote up dollars or tons or kilowatts or spectators, and arrive thereby at a number that might be cause for boasting or lamenting; but you cannot work arithmetic on pain. So much should be obvious in a country that lights candles at the shrine of individualism. We brag to the world about valuing the sovereignty of self. What we actually value is the right of (selected) individuals to accumulate wealth and power at the expense of community and planet.

On the night of his death, John Griffin was cold, abandoned, most likely drunk, and, in the last few minutes, wrapped in flames. He dwelt at the center of an utterly private agony. I can share in it only faintly, through imagination. That is where the drive for change begins, unshielded by statistics or mansions, in empathy with those who suffer.

Questions on Meaning

1. Is this essay predominantly informative or persuasive? What details of Sanders's style lead you to your conclusion?
2. Whom does Sanders blame for the death of the homeless man? Cite the text to support your opinion.

Questions on Rhetorical Strategy and Style

1. Describe the effect of the image "wristlets and anklets of cloth." What does the writer gain by creating this image?
2. Examine the claims Sanders makes in the seventh paragraph, the one beginning, "There is no such calculus. . . ." Which of the claims does he support with evidence in the essay, and which does he ask you to accept without proof?

Writing Assignments

1. What effect did this essay have on you? Write an essay supporting or rebutting Sanders's point of view.
2. "On the night of his death, John Griffin was cold, abandoned, most likely drunk, and, in the last few minutes, wrapped in flames." Why do you think Sanders listed the details of John Griffin's death in exactly this order? Consider other ways of ordering the details and explain the effect of the order Sanders chose.

LANGUAGE AND WRITING

Today's Kids Are, Like, Killing the English Language. Yeah, Right.

Kirk Johnson

Every generation, it seems, has some comment about the younger generation and the butchery it performs on the English language. Adults point to the speech of teenagers and see it as a sign of civilization in decline. School becomes the place where the problem is addressed and teenagers learn to use "proper" language, the language of grownups. In spite of these efforts, the language of youth persists, forcing us to ask the question, "What is language, anyway?" In this article from the August 9, 1998 issue of the New York Times, *Kirk Johnson offers a dynamic view of language, one in which language may be viewed as a logical and creative response to shifting social conditions, the cultural climate, and technological developments.*

1   As a father of two pre-teen boys, I have in the last year or so become a huge fan of the word "duh." This is a word much maligned by educators, linguistic brahmins and purists, but they are all quite wrong.

Duh has elegance. Duh has shades of meaning, even sophistication. Duh and its perfectly paired linguistic partner, "yeah right," are the ideal terms to usher in the millennium and the information age, and to highlight the differences from the stolid old 20th century.

Even my sons might stop me at this point and quash my hyperbole with a quickly dispensed, "Yeah, right, Dad." But hear me out:

"Today's Kids Are, Like, Killing the English Language. Yeah, Right." by Kirk Johnson, reprinted from the *New York Times*, August 9, 1998.

I have become convinced that duh and yeah right have arisen to fill a void in the language because the world has changed. Fewer questions these days can effectively be answered with yes or no, while at the same time, a tidal surge of hype and mindless blather threatens to overwhelm old-fashioned conversation. Duh and yeah right are the cure.

Good old yes and no were fine for their time—the archaic, black and white era of late industrialism that I was born into in the 1950's. The yes-or-no combo was hard and fast and most of all simple: It belonged to the Manichean red-or-dead mentality of the cold war, to manufacturing, to "Father Knows Best" and "It's a Wonderful Life."

5   The information-age future that my 11-year-old twins own is more complicated than yes or no. It's more subtle and supple, more loaded with content and hype and media manipulation than my childhood—or any adult's, living or dead—ever was.

And duh, whatever else it may be, is drenched with content. Between them, duh and yeah-right are capable of dividing all language and thought into an exquisitely differentiated universe. Every statement and every question can be positioned on a gray scale of understatement or overstatement, stupidity or insightfulness, information saturation or yawning emptiness.

And in an era when plain speech has become endangered by the pressures of political correctness, duh and yeah right are matchless tools of savvy, winking sarcasm and skepticism: caustic without being confrontational, incisive without being quite specific.

With duh, you can convey a response, throw in a whole basket full of auxiliary commentary about the question or the statement you're responding to, and insult the speaker all at once! As in this hypothetical exchange:

Parent: "Good morning, son, it's a beautiful day."
10   *Eleven-year-old boy: "Duh."*

And there is a kind of esthetic balance as well. Yeah—right is the yin to duh's yang, the antithesis to duh's empathetic thesis. Where duh is assertive and edgy, a perfect tool for undercutting mindless understatement or insulting repetition, yeah right is laid back, a surfer's cool kind of response to anything overwrought or oversold.

New York, for example, is duh territory, while Los Angeles is yeah—right. Television commercials can be rendered harmless and inert by simply saying, "yeah, right," upon their conclusion. Local television news reports are helped out with a sprinkling of well-placed duhs, at moments of stunning obviousness. And almost any politician's speech cries out for heaping helpings of both at various moments.

Adolescent terms like "like," by contrast, scare me to death. While I have become convinced through observation and personal experimentation that just about any adult of even modest intelligence can figure out how to use duh and yeah right properly, like is different. Like is hard. Like is, like, dangerous.

Marcel Danesi, a professor of linguistics and semiotics at the University of Toronto who has studied the language of youth and who coined the term "pubilect" to describe the dialect of pubescence, said he believes like is in fact altering the structure of the English language, making it more fluid in construction, more like Italian or some other Romance language than good old hard-and-fast Anglo-Saxon. Insert like in the middle of a sentence, he said, and a statement can be turned into a question, a question into an exclamation, an exclamation into a quiet meditation.

15   Consider these hypothetical expressions: "If you're having broccoli for dinner, Mr. Johnson, I'm, like, out of here!" and "I was, like, no way!" and perhaps most startlingly, "He was, like, duh!"

In the broccoli case, like softens the sentence. It's less harsh and confrontational than saying flatly that the serving of an unpalatable vegetable would require a fleeing of the premises.

In the second instance, like functions as a kind of a verbal quotation mark, an announcement that what follows, "no way," is to be heard differently. The quote itself can then be loaded up with any variety of intonation—irony, sarcasm, even self-deprecation—all depending on the delivery.

In the third example—"He was, like, duh!"—like becomes a crucial helping verb for duh, a verbal springboard. (Try saying the sentence without like and it becomes almost incomprehensible.)

But like and duh and yeah right, aside from their purely linguistic virtues, are also in many ways the perfect words to convey the sense of reflected reality that is part of the age we live in. Image manipulation, superficiality, and shallow media culture are, for better or worse, the backdrop of adolescent life.

20   Adults of the yes-or-no era could perhaps grow up firm in their knowledge of what things "are," but in the Age of Duh, with images reflected back from every angle at every waking moment, kids swim

in a sea of what things are "like." Distinguishing what is from what merely seems to be is a required skill of an 11-year-old today; like reflects modern life, and duh and yeah right are the tools with which such a life can be negotiated and mastered.

But there is a concealed paradox in the Age of Duh. The information overload on which it is based is built around the computer, and the computer is, of course, built around—that's right—the good old yes-or-no binary code: Billions of microcircuits all blinking on or off, black or white, current in or current out. Those computers were designed by minds schooled and steeped in the world of yes or no, and perhaps it is not too much of a stretch to imagine my sons' generation, shaped by the broader view of duh, finding another path: binary code with attitude. Besides, most computers I know already seem to have an attitude. Incorporating a little duh would at least give them a sense of humor.

Questions on Meaning

1. "Duh" and "yeah right" have arisen to fill a void in the language. What function do they serve?
2. Explain how "like" differs from "duh" and "yeah right." Why does Johnson say "like" is hard? Dangerous?
3. Why are "yes" and "no" inadequate for the new millennium?

Questions on Rhetorical Strategy and Style

1. What is Johnson's attitude towards pubilect? Cite specific words or phrases that convey his attitude.
2. The conclusion states there is a concealed paradox in the "Age of Duh." Is Johnson shifting his focus or tying the themes of the essay together?
3. Johnson states that "duh" and "yeah right" are the contemporary replacements for "yes" and "no." Illustrate how he uses comparison and contrast to support his claim.

Writing Assignments

1. Write an essay in which you explore your views about the impact of TV or the computer on the English language.
2. Do a study of new words or phrases used by your friends. What void in the language do they fill?
3. Research the uses of "yes" and "no" in the 1950s. Write an essay in which you report on how their meanings have changed.

I Think, Therefore IM

Jennifer Lee

*Jennifer Lee (1976–) was born in New York City. She grad-
uated from Harvard University in 1999 with a degree in
mathematics and economics. While at Harvard she spent a
year at Beijing University on a fellowship studying interna-
tional relations. Lee has received a scholarship from the
Asian American Journalism Association and has interned at*
The Boston Globe, The New York Times, Newsday, The
Wall Street Journal, *and* The Washington Post. *She joined
the staff of* The New York Times *in 2001 as a technology
reporter and began writing for the Metro section the next
year. The following selection on instant-messaging language
originally appeared in the* Times *in September 2002.*

1   Each September Jacqueline Harding prepares a classroom presen- 1
tation on the common writing mistakes she sees in her students'
work.

Ms. Harding, an eighth-grade English teacher at Viking Middle
School in Guernee, Ill., scribbles the words that have plagued generations of school children across her whiteboard:

There. Their. They're.
Your. You're.
To. Too. Two.
Its. It's.

This September, she has added a new list: u, r, ur, b4, wuz, cuz, 2.

When she asked her students how many of them used shortcuts
like them in their writing, Ms. Harding said, she was not surprised
when most of them raised their hands. This, after all, is their online

lingua franca: English adapted for the spitfire conversational style of Internet instant messaging.

Ms. Harding, who has seen such shortcuts creep into student papers over the last two years, said she gave her students a warning: "If I see this in your assignments, I will take points off."

"Kids should know the difference," said Ms. Harding, who decided to address this issue head-on this year. "They should know where to draw the line between formal writing and conversational writing."

As more and more teenagers socialize online, middle school and high school teachers like Ms. Harding are increasingly seeing a breezy form of Internet English jump from e-mail into schoolwork. To their dismay, teachers say that papers are being written with shortened words, improper capitalization and punctuation, and characters like &, $ and @.

Teachers have deducted points, drawn red circles and tsk-tsked at their classes. Yet the errant forms continue. "It stops being funny after you repeat yourself a couple of times," Ms. Harding said.

But teenagers, whose social life can rely as much these days on text communication as the spoken word, say that they use instant-messaging shorthand without thinking about it. They write to one another as much as they write in school, or more.

"You are so used to abbreviating things, you just start doing it unconsciously on schoolwork and reports and other things," said Eve Brecker, 15, a student at Montclair High School in New Jersey.

Ms. Brecker once handed in a midterm exam riddled with instant-messaging shorthand. "I had an hour to write an essay on *Romeo and Juliet*," she said. "I just wanted to finish before my time was up. I was writing fast and carelessly. I spelled 'you' 'u.'" She got a C.

Even terms that cannot be expressed verbally are making their way into papers. Melanie Weaver was stunned by some of the term papers she received from a 10th-grade class she recently taught as part of an internship. "They would be trying to make a point in a paper, they would put a smiley face in the end," said Ms. Weaver, who teaches at Alvernia College in Reading, PA. "If they were presenting an argument and they needed to present an opposite view, they would put a frown."

As Trisha Fogarty, a sixth-grade teacher at Houlton Southside School in Houlton, Maine, puts it, today's students are "Generation Text."

Almost 60 percent of the online population under age 17 uses instant messaging, according to Nielsen/NetRatings. In addition to cellphone text messaging, Weblogs and e-mail, it has become a popular means of flirting, setting up dates, asking for help with homework and keeping in contact with distant friends. The abbreviations are a natural outgrowth of this rapid-fire style of communication.

"They have a social life that centers around typed communication," said Judith S. Donath, a professor at the Massachusetts Institute of Technology's Media Lab who has studied electronic communication. "They have a writing style that has been nurtured in a teenage social milieu."

15   Some teachers see the creeping abbreviations as part of a continuing assault of technology on formal written English. Others take it more lightly, saying that it is just part of the larger arc of language evolution.   15

"To them it's not wrong," said Ms. Harding, who is 28. "It's acceptable because it's in their culture. It's hard enough to teach them the art of formal writing. Now we've got to overcome this new instant-messaging language."

Ms. Harding noted that in some cases the shorthand isn't even shorter. "I understand 'cuz,' but what's with the 'wuz'? It's the same amount of letters as 'was,' so what's the point?" she said.

Deborah Bova, who teaches eighth-grade English at Raymond Park Middle School in Indianapolis, thought her eyesight was failing several years ago when she saw the sentence "B4 we perform, ppl have 2 practice" on a student assignment.

"I thought, 'My God, what is this?' " Ms. Bova said. "Have they lost their minds?"

20   The student was summoned to the board to translate the sentence into standard English: "Before we perform, people have to practice." She realized that the students thought she was out of touch. "It was like 'Get with it, Bova,' " she said. Ms. Bova had a student type up a reference list of translations for common instant-messaging expressions. She posted a copy on the bulletin board by her desk and took another one home to use while grading.   20

Students are sometimes unrepentant.

"They were astonished when I began to point these things out to them," said Henry Assetto, a social studies teacher at Twin Valley High School in Elverson, Pa. "Because I am a history teacher, they did not think a history teacher would be checking up on their grammar or their spelling," said Mr. Assetto, who has been teaching for 34 years.

But Montana Hodgen, 16, another Montclair student, said she was so accustomed to instant-messaging abbreviations that she often read right past them. She proofread a paper last year only to get it returned with the messaging abbreviations circled in red.

"I was so used to reading what my friends wrote to me on Instant Messenger that I didn't even realize that there was something wrong," she said. She said her ability to separate formal and informal English declined the more she used instant messages. "Three years ago, if I had seen that, I would have been 'What is that?' "

25 The spelling checker doesn't always help either, students say. For one, Microsoft Word's squiggly red spell-check lines don't appear beneath single letters and numbers such as u, r, c, 2 and 4. Nor do they catch words which have numbers in them such as "l8r" and "b4" by default.

Teenagers have essentially developed an unconscious "accent" in their typing, Professor Donath said. "They have gotten facile at typing and they are not paying attention."

Teenagers have long pushed the boundaries of spoken language, introducing words that then become passe with adult adoption. Now teenagers are taking charge and pushing the boundaries of written language. For them, expressions like "oic" (oh I see), "nm" (not much), "jk" (just kidding) and "lol" (laughing out loud), "brb" (be right back), "ttyl" (talk to you later) are as standard as conventional English.

"There is no official English language," said Jesse Sheidlower, the North American editor of the *Oxford English Dictionary.* "Language is spread not because anyone dictates any one thing to happen. The decisions are made by the language and the people who use the language."

Some teachers find the new writing style alarming. "First of all, it's very rude, and it's very careless," said Lois Moran, a middle school English teacher at St. Nicholas School in Jersey City.

30 "They should be careful to write properly and not to put these little codes in that they are in such a habit of writing to each other," said Ms. Moran, who has lectured her eighth-grade class on such mistakes.

Others say that the instant-messaging style might simply be a fad, something that students will grow out of. Or they see it as an opportunity to teach students about the evolution of language.

"I turn it into a very positive teachable moment for kids in the class," said Erika V. Karres, an assistant professor at the University of North Carolina at Chapel Hill who trains student teachers. She shows students how English has evolved since Shakespeare's time. "Imagine Langston Hughes's writing in quick texting instead of 'Langston writing,' " she said. "It makes teaching and learning so exciting."

Other teachers encourage students to use messaging shorthand to spark their thinking processes. "When my children are writing first drafts, I don't care how they spell anything, as long as they are writing," said Ms. Fogarty, the sixth-grade teacher from Houlton, Maine. "If this lingo gets their thoughts and ideas onto paper quicker, the more power to them." But during editing and revising, she expects her students to switch to standard English.

Ms. Bova shares the view that instant-messaging language can help free up their creativity. With the help of students, she does not even need the cheat sheet to read the shorthand anymore.

35 "I think it's a plus," she said. "And I would say that with a + sign." 35

Questions on Meaning

1. What are the social and technological conditions that have shaped cyberlingo vocabulary and its uses?
2. What does the term "lingua franca" mean? How does it capture the full significance of the text messaging style of young people?
3. Why, in your opinion, are adults frequently appalled when students use an informal or unconventional style in their writing?

Questions on Rhetorical Strategy and Style

1. Why does Lee open her article with the words Ms. Harding puts on the board each September? What is she trying to suggest to her readers?
2. How does the article adhere to the conventions of the newspaper journalism? Does the writer remain balanced and objective? Explain how.
3. Why does the writer quote the editor of the *Oxford English Dictionary?*

Writing Assignments

1. Why do teachers often seem fussy, and even offended, by their students' use of language? Why are they so insistent about the conventions of standard, edited English? Write an essay that explains to your teachers your experience trying to learn these conventions, and why your language is necessary to your sense of identity.
2. Try the exercise used by Erika Karres, the teacher at the University of North Carolina. Take a poem or any piece of writing and translate it into a quick text version. How does the meaning of it change?

Mother Tongue

Amy Tan

Amy Tan was born in Oakland, California in 1952, several years after her mother and father immigrated from China. She was raised in various cities in the San Francisco Bay Area. When she was eight, her essay, "What the Library Means to Me," won first prize among elementary school participants, for which Tan received a transistor radio and publication in the local newspaper. Upon the deaths of her brother and father in 1967 and 1968 from brain tumors, the family began a haphazard journey through Europe, before settling in Montreux, Switzerland, where Tan graduated in her junior year in 1969.

For the next seven years, Tan attended five schools. She first went to Linfield College in McMinnville, Oregon, and there, on a blind date, met her future husband, Lou DeMattei. She followed him to San Jose, where she enrolled in San Jose City College. She next attended San Jose State University, and, while working two part-time jobs, she became an English honor's students and a President's Scholar, while carrying a semester course load of 21 units. In 1972 she graduated with honors, receiving a B.A. with a double major in English and Linguistics. She was awarded a scholarship to attend the Summer Linguistics Institute at the University of California, Santa Cruz. In 1973, she earned her M.A. in Linguistics, also from San Jose State University, and was then awarded a Graduate Minority Fellowship under the affirmative action program at the University of California, Berkeley, where she enrolled as a doctoral student in linguistics.

First published in *Threepenny Review*, 1990. Copyright © 1990 by Amy Tan.

1　I am not a scholar of English or literature. I cannot give you much more than personal opinions on the English language and its variations in this country or others.

I am a writer. And by that definition, I am someone who has always loved language. I am fascinated by language in daily life. I spend a great deal of my time thinking about the power of language—the way it can evoke an emotion, a visual image, a complex idea, or a simple truth. Language is the tool of my trade. And I use them all—all the Englishes I grew up with.

Recently, I was made keenly aware of the different Englishes I do use. I was giving a talk to a large group of people, the same talk I had already given to half a dozen other groups. The nature of the talk was about my writing, my life, and my book, *The Joy Luck Club.* The talk was going along well enough, until I remembered one major difference that made the whole talk sound wrong. My mother was in the room. And it was perhaps the first time she had heard me give a lengthy speech, using the kind of English I have never used with her. I was saying things like, "The intersection of memory upon imagination" and "There is an aspect of my fiction that relates to thus-and-thus"—a speech filled with carefully wrought grammatical phrases, burdened, it suddenly seemed to me, with nominalized forms, past perfect tenses, conditional phrases, all the forms of standard English that I had learned in school and through books, the forms of English I did not use at home with my mother.

Just last week, I was walking down the street with my mother, and I again found myself conscious of the English I was using, and the English I do use with her. We were talking about the price of new and used furniture and I heard myself saying this: "Not waste money that way." My husband was with us as well, and he didn't notice any switch in my English. And then I realized why. It's because over the twenty years we've been together I've often used that same kind of English with him, and sometimes he even uses it with me. It has become our language of intimacy, a different sort of English that relates to family talk, the language I grew up with.

5　So you'll have some idea of what this family talk I heard sounds like, I'll quote what my mother said during a recent conversation which I videotaped and then transcribed. During this conversation, my mother was talking about a political gangster in Shanghai who had the same last name as her family's, Du, and how the gangster in his early years wanted to be adopted by her family, which was rich by comparison. Later, the gangster became more powerful, far richer than my mother's family, and one day showed up at my mother's wedding to pay his respects. Here's what she said in part:

"Du Yusong having business like fruit stand. Like off the street kind. He is Du like Du Zong—but not Tsung-ming Island people. The local people call putong, the river east side, he belong to that side local people. That man want to ask Du Zong father take him in like become own family. Du Zong father wasn't look down on him, but didn't take seriously, until that man big like become a mafia. Now important person, very hard to inviting him. Chinese way, came only to show respect, don't stay for dinner. Respect for making big celebration, he shows up. Mean gives lots of respect. Chinese custom. Chinese social life that way. If too important won't have to stay too long. He come to my wedding. I didn't see, I heard it. I gone to boy's side, they have YMCA dinner. Chinese age I was nineteen."

You should know that my mother's expressive command of English belies how much she actually understands. She reads the *Forbes* report, listens to *Wall Street Week*, converses daily with her stockbroker, reads all of Shirley MacLaine's books with ease—all kinds of things I can't begin to understand. Yet some of my friends tell me they understand 50 percent of what my mother says. Some say they understand 80 to 90 percent. Some say they understand none of it, as if she were speaking pure Chinese. But to me, my mother's English is perfectly clear, perfectly natural. It's my mother tongue. Her language, as I hear it, is vivid, direct, full of observation and imagery. That was the language that helped shape the way I saw things, expressed things, made sense of the world.

Lately, I've been giving more thought to the kind of English my mother speaks. Like others, I have described it to people as "broken" or "fractured" English. But I wince when I say that. It has always bothered me that I can think of no way to describe it other than "broken," as if it were damaged and needed to be fixed, as if it lacked a certain wholeness and soundness. I've heard other terms used, "limited English," for example. But they seem just as bad, as if everything is limited, including people's perceptions of the limited English speaker.

I know this for a fact, because when I was growing up, my mother's "limited" English limited *my* perception of her. I was ashamed of her English. I believed that her English reflected the quality of what she had to say. That is, because she expressed them imperfectly her thoughts were imperfect. And I had plenty of empirical evidence to support me: the fact that people in department stores, at banks, and at restaurants did not take her seriously, did not give her good service, pretended not to understand her, or even acted as if they did not hear her.

10   My mother has long realized the limitations of her English as well. When I was fifteen, she used to have me call people on the phone to pretend I was she. In this guise, I was forced to ask for information or even to complain and yell at people who had been rude to her. One time it was a call to her stockbroker in New York. She had cashed out her small portfolio and it just so happened we were going to go to New York the next week, our very first trip outside California. I had to get on the phone and say in an adolescent voice that was not very convincing, "This is Mrs. Tan."

And my mother was standing in the back whispering loudly, "Why he don't send me check, already two weeks late. So mad he lie to me, losing me money."

And then I said in perfect English, "Yes, I'm getting rather concerned. You had agreed to send the check two weeks ago, but it hasn't arrived."

Then she began to talk more loudly. "What he want, I come to New York tell him front of his boss, you cheating me?" And I was trying to calm her down, make her be quiet, while telling the stockbroker, "I can't tolerate any more excuses. If I don't receive the check immediately, I am going to have to speak to your manager when I'm in New York next week." And sure enough, the following week there we were in front of this astonished stockbroker, and I was sitting there red-faced and quiet, and my mother, the real Mrs. Tan, was shouting at his boss in her impeccable broken English.

We used a similar routine just five days ago, for a situation that was far less humorous. My mother had gone to the hospital for an appointment, to find out about a benign brain tumor a CAT scan had revealed a month ago. She said she had spoken very good English, her best English, no mistakes. Still, she said, the hospital did not apologize when they said they had lost the CAT scan and she had come for nothing. She said they did not seem to have any sympathy when she told them she was anxious to know the exact diagnosis, since her husband and son had both died of brain tumors. She said they would not give her any more information until the next time and she would have to make another appointment for that. So she said she would not leave until the doctor called her daughter. She wouldn't budge. And when the doctor finally called her daughter, me, who spoke in perfect English—lo and behold—we had assurances the CAT scan would be found, promises that a conference call on Monday would be held, and apologies for any suffering my mother had gone through for a most regrettable mistake.

15   I think my mother's English almost had an effect on limiting my   15
possibilities in life as well. Sociologists and linguists probably will tell you that a person's developing language skills are more influenced by peers. But I do think that the language spoken in the family, especially in immigrant families which are more insular, plays a large role in shaping the language of the child. And I believe that it affected my results on achievement tests, IQ tests, and the SAT. While my English skills were never judged as poor, compared to math, English could not be considered my strong suit. In grade school I did moderately well, getting perhaps B's, sometimes B-pluses, in English and scoring perhaps in the sixtieth or seventieth percentile on achievement tests. But those scores were not good enough to override the opinion that my true abilities lay in math and science, because in those areas I achieved A's and scored in the ninetieth percentile or higher.

This was understandable. Math is precise, there is only one correct answer. Whereas, for me at least, the answers on English tests were always a judgment call, a matter of opinion and personal experience. Those tests were constructed around items like fill-in-the-blank sentence completion, Such as, "Even though Tom was _____, Mary thought he was _____." And the correct answer always seemed to be the most bland combinations of thoughts, for example, "Even though Tom was shy, Mary thought he was charming," with the grammatical structure "even though" limiting the correct answer to some sort of semantic opposites, so you wouldn't get answers like, Even though Tom was foolish, Mary thought he was ridiculous." Well, according to my mother, there were very few limitations as to what Tom could have been and what Mary might have thought of him. So I never did well on tests like that.

The same was true with word analogies, pairs of words in which you were supposed to find some sort of logical, semantic relationship—

for example, "*Sunset* is to *nightfall* as _____ is to _____."
And here you would be presented with a list of four possible pairs, one
of which showed the same kind of relationship: *red* is to *stoplight, bus*
is to *arrival, chills* is to *fever, yawn* is to *boring.* Well, I could never think
that way. I knew what the tests were asking, but I could not block out
of my mind the images already created by the first pair, "*sunset* is to
nightfall"—and I would see a burst of colors against a darkening sky,
the moon rising, the lowering of a curtain of stars. And all the other
pairs of words—red, bus, stoplight, boring—just threw up a mass of
confusing images, making it impossible for me to sort out something
as logical as saying: "A sunset precedes nightfall" is the same as "a chill
precedes a fever." The only way I would have gotten that answer right
would have been to imagine an associative situation, for example, my
being disobedient and staying out past sunset, catching a chill at night,
which turns into feverish pneumonia as punishment, which indeed did
happen to me.

I have been thinking about all this lately, about my mother's English,
about achievement tests. Because lately I've been asked, as a writer,
why there are not more Asian Americans represented in American literature. Why are there few Asian Americans enrolled in creative writing programs? Why do so many Chinese students go into engineering?
Well, these are broad sociological questions I can't begin to answer.
But I have noticed in surveys—in fact, just last week—that Asian students, as a whole, always do significantly better on math achievement
tests than in English. And this makes me think that there are other
Asian American students whose English spoken in the home might
also be described as "broken" or "limited." And perhaps they also have
teachers who are steering them away from writing and into math and
science, which is what happened to me.

Fortunately, I happen to be rebellious in nature and enjoy the
challenge of disproving assumptions made about me. I became an
English major my first year in college, after being enrolled as pre-med.
I started writing nonfiction as a freelancer the week after I was told by
my former boss that writing was my worst skill and I should hone my
talents toward account management.

20 But it wasn't until 1985 that I finally began to write fiction. And 20
at first I wrote using what I thought to be wittily crafted sentences,
sentences that would finally prove I had mastery over the English

language. Here's an example from the first draft of a story that later made its way into *The Joy Luck Club,* but without this line: "That was my mental quandary in its nascent state." A terrible line, which I can barely pronounce.

Fortunately, for reasons I won't get into today, I later decided I should envision a reader for the stories I would write. And the reader I decided upon was my mother, because these were stories about mothers. So with this reader in mind—and in fact she did read my early drafts—I began to write stories using all the Englishes I grew up with: the English I spoke to my mother, which for lack of a better term might be described as "simple"; the English she used with me, which for lack of a better term might be described as "broken"; my translation of her Chinese, which could certainly be described as "watered down"; and what I imagined to be her translation of her Chinese if she could speak in perfect English, her internal language, and for that I sought to preserve the essence, but neither an English nor a Chinese structure. I wanted to capture what language ability tests can never reveal: her intent, her passion, her imagery, the rhythms of her speech and the nature of her thoughts.

Apart from what any critic had to say about my writing, I knew I had succeeded where it counted when my mother finished reading my book and gave me her verdict: "So easy to read."

Questions on Meaning

1. Until near the end of the essay, Tan describes essentially only two "Englishes": the English with which she speaks to others, as in the speech she delivers, and the English of her mother. At the end we learn of a multitude of other Englishes. What are these? What are the differences among them?
2. Why was Tan ashamed of her mother's English when she was growing up?
3. What does Tan have to say about her math scores being higher than her language scores?

Questions on Rhetorical Strategy and Style

4. Tan uses the writing strategy of narration to reveal how others reacted to her mother's language skills, such as the treatment she received at the hospital. Reread that scene and explain how it effectively develops Tan's point.
5. Tan says that she wanted in her writing to capture her mother's "intent, her passion, her imagery, the rhythms of her speech and the nature of her thoughts." Evaluate this essay by this standard: do we get a glimpse of her mother's character here? How does Tan use language in this essay to capture a small part of her mother?

Writing Assignments

1. Tan makes the point that teachers may be steering Asian American students into math and science because their language scores may mistakenly be suggesting they have lower aptitude in studies involving language. Could such "steering" by teachers and guidance counselors be faulty with other students as well? Think of some other examples of situations in which test scores could give false impressions about a person's natural abilities and aptitudes.
2. Tan describes how people judged her mother as a result of her "broken English." What other ways do people judge strangers by appearances? Do clothing and physical appearance give true insight into what a person is like? Write an essay in which you explore the issue of how we come to know what people are like and the extent to which it is meaningful to make assumptions based on how people look and sound.

3. Tan explains at length how she never understood word analogy tests because her mind just did not work that way. Is this more than just a matter of using English? Are there differences in how people think that can throw off such responses to standardized tests, such as those used to measure intelligence? Write an essay in which you explain your ideas, based on your own experience, about whether standardized tests accurately measure people's abilities and aptitudes.

⌒ WHAT DID U $@Y? ONLINE ⌒
LANGUAGE FINDS ITS VOICE

Christopher Rhoads

August 23, 2007

TEh INTeRn3T i5 THr3@+EN1N9 t0 Ch@n93 thE W4Y wE $p34k.
(Translation: The Internet is threatening to change the way we speak.)

1 For years, heavy users of Internet games and chat groups have conversed in their own written language, often indecipherable to outsiders. Now, some of those online words are gaining currency in popular culture—even in spoken form.

Online gamers use "pwn" to describe annihilating an opponent, or owning them. The word came from misspelling "own" by gamers typing quickly and striking the letter P instead of the neighboring letter O. Other words substitute symbols or numbers for similar-looking letters, such as the number 3 for the letter E. The language is sometimes called elite speak, or leetspeak, written as l33t 5p34k.

There is no standardized code. The letter A, for example, can have several replacements, including 4, /\, @ , /-\, ^, and aye.

As the Internet becomes more prevalent, leetspeak, including acronyms that used to appear only in text messages like "LOL" for laughing out loud, is finding a voice.

5 "I pone you, you're going down dude, lawl!" is how Johnathan Wendel says he likes to taunt opponents in person at online gaming tournaments. Pone is how he pronounces "pwn," and lawl is how

---

Christopher Rhoads is a prolific writer for the *Wall Street Journal*, for which he wrote this article.

Reprinted by permission from the *Wall Street Journal*, August 23, 2007.

"LOL" usually sounds when spoken. Mr. Wendel, 26 years old, has earned more than $500,000 in recent years by winning championships in Internet games like Quake 3 and Alien vs. Predator 2. His screen name is Fatal1ty.

During the televised World Series of Poker last year, one player, remarking on a deft move, told an opponent that he had been "poned." In an episode of the animated TV show "South Park," one of the characters shouted during an online game, "Looks like you're about to get poned, yeah!" Another character later marveled, "That was such an uber-ponage."

One problem with speaking in such code: there is little agreement on pronunciation.

Jarett Cale, the 29-year-old star of an Internet video series called "Pure Pwnage," enunciates the title "pure own-age." This is correct since "pwn" was originally a typo, he argues, and sounds "a lot cooler." But many of the show's fans, which he estimates at around three million, prefer to say pone-age, he acknowledges. Others pronounce it poon, puh-own, pun or pwone.

"I think we're probably losing the war," says Mr. Cale, whose character on the show, Jeremy, likes to wear a black T-shirt with the inscription, "I pwn n00bs." (That, for the uninitiated, means "I own newbies," or amateurs.)

Those who utter the term "teh" are also split. A common online misspelling of "the," "teh" has come to mean "very" when placed in front of an adjective—such as "tehcool" for "very cool." Some pronounce it tuh, others tay.

The words' growing offline popularity has stoked the ire of linguists, parents and others who denounce them as part of a broader debasement of the English language.

"There used to be a time when people cared about how they spoke and wrote," laments Robert Hartwell Fiske, who has written or edited several books on proper English usage, including one on overused words titled "The Dimwit's Dictionary."

When a reader of his online journal, called the Vocabula Review, proposed "leet," as in leetspeak, for his list of best words, Mr. Fiske rejected it.

"Leet: slang for 'good' or 'great,' apparently, and 'idiotic,' certainly," he wrote on the Vocabula Web site. "Leet" is in dictionaries with other meanings, including a soft-finned fish.

15   Lake Superior State University, in Sault Ste. Marie, Mich., this year   15
included "pwn" on its annual list of banned words and phrases—those it
considers misused, overly used and just plain useless. Others on the list
included "awesome" and "Gitmo" (shorthand for Guantanamo Bay).

Some suggest such verbal creations are nothing new and are inte-
gral to how language evolves.

Gail Kern Paster, director of the Folger Shakespeare Library in
Washington, D.C., has reason to believe that a certain English poet
and playwright would cheer the latest linguistic leap. Just as the rise of
the printed word and the theater spurred many new expressions during Shakespeare's time, the computer revolution, she notes, has neces-
sitated its own vocabulary—like "logging in" and "Web site."

"The issue of correctness didn't bother him," says Ms. Paster. "He
loved to play with language." As for leet, "He would say, 'Bring it on,'
absolutely."

The word "OK," one of the most widely used words in many lan-
guages, first appeared in a Boston newspaper in 1839 as an abbreviation
for "oll korrect," according to Allan Metcalf, a professor of English at
MacMurray College in Jacksonville, Ill. Other abbreviations, such as
O.F.M. for our first men, referring—sometimes sarcastically—to a
community's leading citizens, also became briefly popular in Boston
newspapers at the time, says Mr. Metcalf.

20   The Internet is not the first technological advancement to   20
change the way language is used. The telegraph required people to
communicate "with lots of dots and dashes and abbreviations," says
Mr. Metcalf. "Since it charged by the word, you compressed your
message as much as possible—grammar be damned."

Some of those words, like SOS, the popular call for help, have
survived from their telegraph-era origins.

Leetspeak first became popular in the 1980s among hackers and
those adept enough to gain access to an early form of online chat
forums called bulletin boards. These "elite" users developed leetspeak,
occasionally to conceal their hacking plans or elude text filters. (It still
has that use for some: "pr0n" is leetspeak for pornography.)

But leetspeak's growing appeal, and use among the un-cool,
could undermine it. "Now moms are saying, 'LOL,' so that takes
away from it," says Mr. Cale of the Internet show "Pure Pwnage."

A couple of years ago, Katherine Blashki, a professor of new
media studies, didn't understand some of the words used by her

students at Deakin University in Melbourne, Australia. Her subsequent, semester-long research on the subject found their use of leetspeak stemmed partly from wanting to find faster ways to express themselves online. As with other forms of jargon, it also enhanced a sense of belonging to a community, she says.

25 "It's ultimately about creating a secret language that can differentiate them from others, like parents," says Ms. Blashki. "That's part of being a teenager."

She presented her work at a conference in Spain and has since written nearly a dozen research papers on the topic. She admits she hasn't received much grant funding for her work. "My peers were aghast," she says.

Despite their facility with the new language, some leet fans insist that good grammar is still important.

Mr. Wendel, the online gamer, says he makes a point of using proper capitalization and punctuation in his online missives during competition. "It's always a last resort," says Mr. Wendel. "If you lose you can say, 'At least I can spell.'"

MULTICULTURALISM AND DIVERSITY

The Struggle to Be an All-American Girl

Elizabeth Wong

Elizabeth Wong, a playwright and television writer, grew up in Chinatown in Los Angeles. Although she resisted, her mother insisted that she learn the Chinese language and culture when she was in grade school. Educated at the University of Southern California (1980) and New York University (1991), Wong has worked as a reporter and taught in the theater department at Bowdoin College. In this essay, which was first published in the Los Angeles Times, *Wong recounts her childhood rebellion against learning Chinese and her adult regret of her assimilation into American culture.*

1 It's still there, the Chinese school on Yale Street where my brother and I used to go. Despite the new coat of paint and the high wire fence, the school I knew 10 years ago remains remarkably, stoically the same.

Every day at 5 P.M., instead of playing with our fourth- and fifth-grade friends or sneaking out to the empty lot to hunt ghosts and animal bones, my brother and I had to go to Chinese school. No amount of kicking, screaming, or pleading could dissuade my mother, who was solidly determined to have us learn the language of our heritage.

Forcibly, she walked us the seven long, hilly blocks from our home to school, depositing our defiant tearful faces before the stern principal. My only memory of him is that he swayed on his heels like a palm tree, and he always clasped his impatient twitching hands behind his back. I recognized him as a repressed maniacal child killer, and knew that if we ever saw his hands we'd be in big trouble.

Originally appeared in the *Los Angeles Times.*

We all sat in little chairs in an empty auditorium. The room smelled like Chinese medicine, an imported faraway mustiness. Like ancient mothballs or dirty closets. I hated that smell. I favored crisp new scents. Like the soft French perfume that my American teacher wore in public school.

5   There was a stage far to the right, flanked by an American flag and the flag of the Nationalist Republic of China, which was also red, white and blue but not as pretty.   5

Although the emphasis at the school was mainly language—speaking, reading, writing—the lessons always began with an exercise in politeness. With the entrance of the teacher, the best student would tap a bell and everyone would get up, kowtow, and chant, "Sing san ho," the phonetic for "How are you, teacher?"

Being ten years old, I had better things to learn than ideographs copied painstakingly in lines that ran right to left from the tip of a *moc but,* a real ink pen that had to be held in an awkward way if blotches were to be avoided. After all, I could do the multiplication tables, name the satellites of Mars, and write reports on *Little Women* and *Black Beauty.* Nancy Drew, my favorite book heroine, never spoke Chinese.

The language was a source of embarrassment. More times than not, I had tried to disassociate myself from the nagging loud voice that followed me wherever I wandered in the nearby American supermarket outside Chinatown. The voice belonged to my grandmother, a fragile woman in her seventies who could outshout the best of the street vendors. Her humor was raunchy, her Chinese rhythmless, patternless. It was quick, it was loud, it was unbeautiful. It was not like the quiet, lilting romance of French or the gentle refinement of the American South. Chinese sounded pedestrian. Public.

In Chinatown, the comings and goings of hundreds of Chinese on their daily tasks sounded chaotic and frenzied. I did not want to be thought of as mad, as talking gibberish. When I spoke English, people nodded at me, smiled sweetly, said encouraging words. Even the people in my culture would cluck and say that I'd do well in life. "My, doesn't she move her lips fast," they would say, meaning that I'd be able to keep up with the world outside Chinatown.

10   My brother was even more fanatical than I about speaking English. He was especially hard on my mother, criticizing her, often cruelly, for her pidgin speech—smatterings of Chinese scattered like chop   10

suey in her conversation. "It's not 'What it is,' Mom," he'd say in exasperation. "It's 'What *is* it, what *is* it, what *is* it!' " Sometimes Mom might leave out an occasional "the" or "a," or perhaps a verb of being. He would stop her in mid-sentence: "Say it again, Mom. Say it right." When he tripped over his own tongue, he'd blame it on her: "See, Mom, it's all your fault. You set a bad example."

What infuriated my mother most was when my brother cornered her on her consonants, especially "r." My father had played a cruel joke on Mom by assigning her an American name that her tongue wouldn't allow her to say. No matter how hard she tried, "Ruth" always ended up "Luth" or "Roof."

After two years of writing with a *moc but* and reciting words with multiples of meanings, I finally was granted a cultural divorce. I was permitted to stop Chinese school.

I thought of myself as multicultural. I preferred tacos to egg rolls; I enjoyed Cinco de Mayo[1] more than Chinese New Year.

At last, I was one of you; I wasn't one of them.

Sadly, I still am.

---

[1]Fifth of May, Mexican national holiday marking Mexico's victory over France at Puebla in 1862.

Questions on Meaning

1. Why did Wong's mother want her to go to Chinese school? What does she know about Chinese school now that she didn't realize when she was in grade school?
2. Why was the Chinese language a source of embarrassment for Wong?
3. What was the "cruel joke" Wong's father had played on her mother?

Questions on Rhetorical Strategy and Style

1. How does Wong compare and contrast her Chinese school with her American school? Why did she prefer the American school?
2. Sound plays a major role in many of Wong's descriptions. Identify the various sounds that have become part of her memory of Chinese school, her grandmother, and Chinatown. Explain why she remembers these sounds as being pleasurable or discordant.
3. How does Wong's final sentence change the tone of the entire essay? What is the irony of her title as revealed by this statement?

Writing Assignments

1. Describe some objectionable activity you were forced to do as a child because some adult authority figure knew it was good for you. Why did you resist? What was the long-term impact of the activity? What would you do now in the same circumstance with your own children?
2. Write an essay on assimilation. How important do you think it is for immigrants to become imbued in American culture? How much of their own culture should newcomers to this country retain? What conflicts between the past and the future does assimilation create?

The Handicap of Definition

William Raspberry

William Raspberry (1935–) was born in Okolona, Mississippi. His mother was an English teacher and poet, his father a shop teacher. After graduating from Indiana Central College, he worked for the Indianapolis Recorder *as a reporter and editor, spent two years in the army, and then joined the* Washington Post. *Raspberry was awarded the Capital Press Club "Journalist of the Year" award in 1965 for his coverage of the Watts (Los Angeles) race riots. He has written a syndicated column, originating at the* Washington Post, *since 1971. A collection of his columns appears in* Looking Backward at Us *(1991). Raspberry's perspectives reflect the respect for knowledge he gained from his parents, the segregated world in which he lived as a youth, and the civil rights movement. In this essay, which was published as a column in 1982, Raspberry challenges blacks—and society—to broaden the definition of "blackness" from strictly sports and entertainment skills.*

1   I know all about bad schools, mean politicians, economic deprivation   1
and racism. Still, it occurs to me that one of the heaviest burdens
black Americans—and black children in particular—have to bear is
the handicap of definition: the question of what it means to be black.

Let me explain quickly what I mean. If a basketball fan says that
the Boston Celtics' Larry Bird plays "black," the fan intends it—and
Bird probably accepts it—as a compliment. Tell pop singer Tom Jones
he moves "black" and he might grin in appreciation. Say to Teena
Marie or the Average White Band that they sound "black" and they'll
thank you.

But name one pursuit, aside from athletics, entertainment or sexual performance, in which a white practitioner will feel complimented to be told he does it "black." Tell a white broadcaster he talks "black" and he'll sign up for diction lessons. Tell a white reporter he writes "black" and he'll take a writing course. Tell a white lawyer he reasons "black" and he might sue you for slander.

What we have here is a tragically limited definition of blackness, and it isn't only white people who buy it.

Think of all the ways black children can put one another down with charges of "whiteness." For many of these children, hard study and hard work are "white." Trying to please a teacher might be criticized as acting "white." Speaking correct English is "white." Scrimping today in the interest of tomorrow's goals is "white." Educational toys and games are "white."

An incredible array of habits and attitudes that are conducive to success in business, in academia, in the nonentertainment professions are likely to be thought of as somehow "white." Even economic success, unless it involves such "black" undertakings as numbers banking, is defined as "white."

And the results are devastating. I wouldn't deny that blacks often are better entertainers and athletes. My point is the harm that comes from too narrow a definition of what is black.

One reason black youngsters tend to do better at basketball, for instance, is that they assume they can learn to do it well, and so they practice constantly to prove themselves right.

Wouldn't it be wonderful if we could infect black children with the notion that excellence in math is "black" rather than white, or possibly Chinese? Wouldn't it be of enormous value if we could create the myth that morality, strong families, determination, courage and love of learning are traits brought by slaves from Mother Africa and therefore quintessentially black?

There is no doubt in my mind that most black youngsters could develop their mathematical reasoning, their elocution and their attitudes the way they develop their jump shots and their dance steps: by the combination of sustained, enthusiastic practice and the unquestioned belief that they can do it.

In one sense, what I am talking about is the importance of developing positive ethnic traditions. Maybe Jews have an innate talent for communication; maybe the Chinese are born with a gift for

79

mathematical reasoning; maybe blacks are naturally blessed with athletic grace. I doubt it. What is at work, I suspect, is assumption, inculcated early in their lives, that this is a thing our people do well.

Unfortunately, many of the things about which blacks make this assumption are things that do not contribute to their career success—except for that handful of the truly gifted who can make it as entertainers and athletes. And many of the things we concede to whites are the things that are essential to economic security.

So it is with a number of assumptions black youngsters make about what it is to be a "man": physical aggressiveness, sexual prowess, the refusal to submit to authority. The prisons are full of people who, by this perverted definition, are unmistakably men.

But the real problem is not so much that the things defined as "black" are negative. The problem is that the definition is much too narrow.

15   Somehow, we have to make our children understand that they are   15 intelligent, competent people, capable of doing whatever they put their minds to and making it in the American mainstream, not just in a black subculture.

What we seem to be doing, instead, is raising up yet another generation of young blacks who will be failures—by definition.

Questions on Meaning

1. What does Raspberry mean by the "handicap of definition"? What is his premise about this definition?
2. Raspberry feels that blacks can achieve success in many fields other than athletics and entertainment. What does he state that blacks must do to achieve this success? How do these requirements for success compare with what they must do to achieve success in athletics and entertainment?
3. What are the "white" social stigmas for black children that are attached to competence and success? How do these cultural pressures impede their growth and development?

Questions on Rhetorical Strategy and Style

1. Find where Raspberry uses comparison and contrast to refute society's ethnic stereotypes. How do you think these stereotypes have developed? Explain how, in your experience, they are reinforced by educators.
2. How does Raspberry use cause and effect to explain the imprisonment of so many black men? How does television—sports broadcasts, MTV, and advertising, for example—help perpetuate the destructive self-image of young blacks?

Writing Assignments

1. The "handicap of definition" applies also to women. Identify fields in which women historically have had limited opportunity (and success). How have those limitations changed in recent years?
2. Write an essay on an incident in your life in which you were told you shouldn't pursue something because "you aren't good at that," or "no one in our family ever does that," or "that just isn't something that [boys or girls] do." What did it do to your self-image? How did it affect your belief in what you *could* do? What was your reaction?

THE HUMAN CULTURE

Lemuel Canady Jr.

In his essay, "The Handicap of Definition," William Raspberry talks about what it means to live with the definition of 'being black.' He talks about acting black, or playing black, or sounding black when it comes to sports or entertainment. Mr. Raspberry discusses the fact that, when it comes to academia or successful business, any term that has to do with the future of success is to 'act white.' He believes that we need to broaden our terms on what it means to be black. While I believe this—that the world in general needs to broaden what blackness means—is true, I think we need to take this further. I believe we should no longer label our actions, our proficiencies with a color or race.

Growing up, I'd heard quite a few definitions on what it means to be black, what we're good at and what we normally stay away from as a people in general. Though I believe it's because of my parents that I've really never listened to what's considered 'normal,' a good part of that has to do with growing up in a military family and moving around most of my young life. I was around six years old when my family finally settled in Alexandria Virginia, just outside of Washington DC. I spent the first six years of my life traveling around the country and the world, before I'd ever heard the term that someone, or something was acting 'black' in a positive or negative sense. My parents also didn't fit these stereotypes. My parents were the first generation to graduate with a college degree or even further, to earn Master's degrees and Doctorate's. They valued higher education more than social standards. But it also meant that I was encouraged to follow what I wanted to do, what I wanted to be, and not let anyone tell me otherwise.

Lemuel Canady Jr. wrote this essay for his WRIT 117 class, in response to William Raspberry's essay "The Handicap of Definition," in Fall 2007.

82

Unfortunately, this also makes interacting with other members of my family harder, because I don't fit the definition of 'black.' I listen to heavy metal music, play video games, and program computers. I wear dark colors, and I spend more time working my character designs than I do following pop culture, so when it comes time to visit or receive visitors in a 'family reunion' setting, I stick out like a sore thumb. I tend to avoid those sorts of functions, because I really never have any more in common than a 'hello' to a few people, who stare at me glassy eyed after asking me what I've been doing with myself.

How about black culture in general? There's a silent definition out there of how we should act as a culture, or how we should act as a people, and I've noticed that I don't fit at all. In fact, more often than not, I'm told that I act white, or that I'm trying to act white. Is this because I tend not to listen to rap and R&B? Is this because my parents never let me use 'slang' when I was growing up? Is it because I'm trying to be successful that I've been deemed to 'act white'? I don't think I'll ever really understand. But it leaves me in this awkward place where I tend not to be given a chance with African American culture, unfortunately.

5   What does it really mean to act black, or act white? Does it really matter? When I hear or read what it means to 'act black,' I see it all now labeled as urban culture. The clothing, the music, the sports, you don't just see black men and women, boys and girls doing it anymore. You see people from all walks of life. What started as a racially-based culture has grown into something bigger. It's grown into city culture, urban culture; it's bypassed race and color to stand for something completely different altogether. But I don't see myself as black, or my friends as white, black, or any other mixture within. I see them as fellow artists and computer addicts. I see them as urbanites, and metal heads, geeks and weirdoes. I see myself, my friends, and others that I come across as human, and in that, there's no handicap of definition.

GOIN' GANGSTA, CHOOSIN' CHOLITA: TEENS TODAY "CLAIM" A RACIAL IDENTITY

Nell Bernstein

Her lipstick is dark, the lip liner even darker, nearly black. In baggy pants, a blue plaid Pendleton, her bangs pulled back tight off her forehead, 15-year-old April is a perfect cholita, a Mexican gangsta girl.

But April Miller is Anglo. "And I don't like it!" she complains. "I'd rather be Mexican."

April's father wanders into the family room of their home in San Leandro, California, a suburb near Oakland. "Hey, cholita," he teases. "Go get a suntan. We'll put you in a barrio and see how much you like it."

A large, sandy-haired man with "April" tattooed on one arm and "Kelly"—the name of his older daughter—on the other, Miller spent 21 years working in a San Leandro glass factory that shut down and moved to Mexico a couple of years ago. He recently got a job in another factory, but he expects NAFTA to swallow that one, too.

"Sooner or later we'll all get nailed," he says. "Just another stab in the back of the American middle class."

Later, April gets her revenge: "Hey, Mr. White Man's Last Stand," she teases. "Wait till you see how well I manage my welfare check. You'll be asking me for money."

Nell Bernstein has published articles and essays in several popular magazines and has written one book, *All Alone in the World: Children of Incarcerated Parents.* She wrote this essay for the *Utne* Reader in 1995.

A once almost exclusively white, now increasingly Latin and black working-class suburb, San Leandro borders on predominantly black East Oakland. For decades, the boundary was strictly policed and practically impermeable. In 1970 April Miller's hometown was 97 percent white. By 1990 San Leandro was 65 percent white, 6 percent black, 15 percent Hispanic, and 13 percent Asian or Pacific Islander. With minorities moving into suburbs in growing numbers and cities becoming ever more diverse, the boundary between city and suburb is dissolving, and suburban teenagers are changing with the times.

In April's bedroom, her past and present selves lie in layers, the pink walls of girlhood almost obscured, Guns N' Roses and Pearl Jam posters overlaid by rappers Paris and Ice Cube. "I don't have a big enough attitude to be a black girl," says April, explaining her current choice of ethnic identification.

What matters is that she thinks the choice is hers. For April and her friends, identity is not a matter of where you come from, what you were born into, what color your skin is. It's what you wear, the music you listen to, the words you use—everything to which you pledge allegiance, no matter how fleetingly.

10 The hybridization of American teens has become talk show fodder, 10 with "wiggers"—white kids who dress and talk "black"—appearing on TV in full gangsta regalia. In Indiana a group of white high school girls raised a national stir when they triggered an imitation race war at their virtually all white high school last fall simply by dressing "black."

In many parts of the country, it's television and radio, not neighbors, that introduce teens to the allure of ethnic difference. But in California, which demographers predict will be the first state with no racial majority by the year 2000, the influences are more immediate. The California public schools are the most diverse in the country: 42 percent white, 36 percent Hispanic, 9 percent black, 8 percent Asian.

Sometimes young people fight over their differences. Students at virtually any school in the Bay Area can recount the details of at least one "race riot" in which a conflict between individuals escalated into a battle between their clans. More often, though, teens would rather join than fight. Adolescence, after all, is the period when you're most inclined to mimic the power closest at hand, from stealing your older sister's clothes to copying the ruling clique at school.

White skaters and Mexican would-be gangbangers listen to gangsta rap and call each other "nigga" as term of endearment; white girls sometimes affect Spanish accents; blond cheerleaders claim Cherokee ancestors.

"Claiming" is the central concept here. A Vietnamese teen in Hayward, another Oakland suburb, "claims" Oakland—and by implication blackness—because he lived there as a child. A law-abiding white kid "claims" a Mexican gang he says he hangs with. A brown-skinned girl with a Mexican father and a white mother "claims" her Mexican side, while her fair-skinned sister "claims" white. The word comes up over and over, as if identity were territory, the self a kind of turf.

15   At a restaurant in a minimall in Hayward, Nicole Huffstutler, 13, sits with her friends and describes herself as "Indian, German, French, Welsh, and, um . . . American": "If somebody says anything like 'Yeah, you're just a peckerwood,' I'll walk up and I'll say 'white pride!' 'Cause I'm proud of my race, and I wouldn't wanna be any other race."

"Claiming" white has become a matter of principle for Heather, too, who says she's "sick of the majority looking at us like we're less than them." (Hayward schools were 51 percent white in 1990, down from 77 percent in 1980, and whites are now the minority in many schools.)

Asked if she knows that nonwhites have not traditionally been referred to as "the majority" in America, Heather gets exasperated: "I hear that all the time, every day. They say, 'Well, you guys controlled us for many years, and it's time for us to control you.' Every day."

When Jennifer Vargas—a small, brown-skinned girl in purple jeans who quietly eats her salad while Heather talks—softly announces that she's "mostly Mexican," she gets in trouble with her friends.

"No, you're not!" scolds Heather.

20   "I'm mostly Indian and Mexican," Jennifer continues, flatly. "I'm very little . . . I'm mostly . . ."

"Your mom's white!" Nicole reminds her sharply. "She has blond hair."

"That's what I mean," Nicole adds. "People think that white is a bad thing. They think that white is a bad race. So she's trying to claim more Mexican than white."

"I have very little white in me," Jennifer repeats. "I have mostly my dad's side, 'cause I look like him and stuff. And most of my friends think that me and my brother and sister aren't related, 'cause they look more like my mom."

"But you guys are all the same race, you just look different," Nicole insists. She stops eating and frowns. "OK, you're half and half each what your parents have. So you're equal as your brother and sister, you just look different. And you should be proud of what you are—every little piece and bit of what you are. Even if you were Afghan or whatever, you should be proud of it."

25   Will Mosley, Heather's 17-year-old brother, says he and his friends listen to rap groups like Compton's Most Wanted, NWA, and Above the Law because they "sing about life"—that is, what happens in Oakland, Los Angeles, anyplace but where Will is sitting today, an empty Round Table Pizza in a minimall.

"No matter what race you are," Will says, "if you live like we do, then that's the kind of music you like."

And how do they live?

"We don't live bad or anything," Will admits. "We live in a pretty good neighborhood, there's no violence or crime. I was just . . . we're just city people, I guess."

Will and his friend Adolfo Garcia, 16, say they've outgrown trying to be something they're not. "When I was 11 or 12," Will says, "I thought I was becoming a big gangsta and stuff. Because I liked that music, and thought it was the coolest, I wanted to become that. I wore big clothes, like you wear in jail. But then I kind of woke up. I looked at myself and thought, 'Who am I trying to be?'"

30   They may have outgrown blatant mimicry, but Will and his friends remain convinced that they can live in a suburban tract house with a well-kept lawn on a tree-lined street in "not a bad neighborhood" and still call themselves "city" people on the basis of musical tastes. "City" for these young people means crime, graffiti, drugs. The kids are law-abiding, but these activities connote what Will admiringly calls "action." With pride in his voice, Will predicts that "in a couple of years, Hayward will be like Oakland. It's starting to get more known, because of crime and things. I think it'll be bigger, more things happening, more crime, more graffiti, stealing cars."

"That's good," chimes in 15-year-old Matt Jenkins whose new beeper—an item that once connoted gangsta chic but now means little more than an active social life—goes off periodically. "More fun."

The three young men imagine with disdain life in a gangsta-free zone. "Too bland, too boring," Adolfo says. "You have to have something going on. You can't just have everyday life."

"Mowing your lawn," Matt sneers.

"Like Beaver Cleaver's house," Adolfo adds. "It's too clean out here."

35 Not only white kids believe that identity is a matter of choice or taste, or that the power of "claiming" can transcend ethnicity. The Manor Park Locos—a group of mostly Mexican-Americans who hang out in San Leandro's Manor Park—say they descend from the Manor Lords, tough white guys who ruled the neighborhood a generation ago.

They "are like our . . . uncles and dads, the older generation," says Jesse Martinez, 14. "We're what they were when they were around, except we're Mexican."

"There's three generations," says Oso, Jesse's younger brother. "There's Manor Lords, Manor Park Locos, and Manor Park Pee Wees." The Pee Wees consist mainly of the Locos' younger brothers, eager kids who circle the older boys on bikes and brag about "punking people."

Unlike Will Mosley, the Locos find little glamour in city life. They survey the changing suburban landscape and see not "action" or "more fun" but frightening decline. Though most of them are not yet 18, the Locos are already nostalgic, longing for a Beaver Cleaver past that white kids who mimic them would scoff at.

Walking through nearly empty Manor Park, with its eucalyptus stands, its softball diamond and tennis courts, Jesse's friend Alex, the only Asian in the group, waves his arms in a gesture of futility. "A few years ago, every bench was filled," he says. "Now no one comes here. I guess it's because of everything that's going on. My parents paid a lot for this house, and I want it to be nice for them. I just hope this doesn't turn into Oakland."

40 Glancing across the park at April Miller's street, Jesse says he knows what the white cholitas are about. "It's not a racial thing," he explains. "It's just all the most popular people out here are Mexican. We're just the gangstas that everyone knows. I guess those girls wanna be known."

Not every young Californian embraces the new racial hybridism. Andrea Jones, 20, an African-American who grew up in the Bay Area suburbs of Union City and Hayward, is unimpressed by what she sees mainly as shallow mimicry. "It's full of posers out here," she says.

"When *Boyz N the Hood* came out on video, it was sold out for weeks. The boys all wanna be black, the girls all wanna be Mexican. It's the glamour."

Driving down the quiet, shaded streets of her old neighborhood in Union City, Andrea spots two white preteen boys in Raiders jackets and hugely baggy pants strutting erratically down the empty sidewalk. "Look at them," she says. "Dislocated."

She knows why. "In a lot of these schools out here, it's hard being white." she says. "I don't think these kids were prepared for the backlash that is going on, all the pride now in people of color's ethnicity, and our boldness with it. They have nothing like that, no identity, nothing they can say they're proud of.

"So they latch onto their great-grandmother who's a Cherokee, or they take on the most stereotypical aspects of being black or Mexican. It's beautiful to appreciate different aspects of other people's culture—that's like the dream of what the 21st century should be. But to garnish yourself with pop culture stereotypes just to blend—that's really sad."

45 Roland Krevocheza, 18, graduated last year from Arroyo High 45
School in San Leandro. He is Mexican on his mother's side, Eastern European on his father's. In the new hierarchies, it may be mixed kids like Roland who have the hardest time finding their place, even as their numbers grow. (One in five marriages in California is between people of different races.) They can always be called "wannabes," no matter what they claim.

"I'll state all my nationalities," Roland says. But he takes a greater interest in his father's side, his Ukrainian, Romanian, and Czech ancestors. "It's more unique," he explains. "Mexican culture is all around me. We eat Mexican food all the time, I hear stories from my grandmother. I see the low-riders and stuff. I'm already part of it. I'm not trying to be; I am."

His darker-skinned brother "says he's not proud to be white," Roland adds. "He calls me 'Mr. Nazi.'" In the room the two share, the American flags and the reproduction of the Bill of Rights are Roland's; the Public Enemy poster belongs to his brother.

Roland has good reason to mistrust gangsta attitudes. In his junior year in high school, he was one of several Arroyo students who were beaten up outside the school at lunchtime by a group of Samoans who came in cars from Oakland. Roland wound up with a split lip, a concussion, and a broken tailbone. Later he was told that the assault was "gang-related"—that the Samoans were beating up anyone wearing red.

"Rappers, I don't like them," Roland says. "I think they're a bad influence on kids. It makes kids think they're all tough and bad."

50 Those who, like Roland, dismiss the gangsta and cholo styles as affectations can point to the fact that several companies market over-priced knockoffs of "ghetto wear" targeted at teens.   50

But there's also something going on out here that transcends ado-lescent faddishness and pop culture exoticism. When white kids call their parents "racist" for nagging them about their baggy pants; when they learn Spanish to talk to their boyfriends; when Mexican-American boys feel themselves descended in spirit from white "uncles"; when children of mixed marriages insist that they are what-ever race they say they are, all of them are more than just confused.

They're inching toward what Andrea Jones calls "the dream of what the 21st century should be." In the ever more diverse communi-ties of Northern California, they're also facing the complicated reality of what their 21st century will be.

Meanwhile, in the living room of the Miller family's San Leandro home, the argument continues unabated. "You don't know what you are," April's father has told her more than once. But she just keeps on telling him he doesn't know what time it is.

WEALTH AND POVERTY

THE HIDDEN LIFE OF
BOTTLED WATER

Liza Gross

A mericans used to turn on their faucets when they craved a drink of clear, cool water. Today, concerned about the safety of water supplies, they're turning to the bottle. Consumers spent more than $4 billion on bottled water last year, establishing the fount of all life as a certifiably hot commodity. But is bottled really better?

You might think a mountain stream on the label offers some clue to the contents. But sometimes, to paraphrase Freud, a bottle is just a bottle. "Mountain water could be anything," warns Connie Crawley, a health and nutrition specialist at the University of Georgia. "Unless the label says it comes from a specific source, when the manufacturer says 'bottled at the source,' the source could be the tap."

Yosemite brand water comes not from a bucolic mountain spring but from deep wells in the undeniably less-picturesque Los Angeles suburbs, and Everest sells water drawn from a municipal source in Corpus Christi, Texas-a far cry from the pristine glacial peaks suggested by its name. As long as producers meet the FDA's standards for "distilled" or "purified" water, they don't have to disclose the source.

Even if the water does come from a spring, what's in that portable potable may be less safe than what comes out of your tap. Bottled water must meet the same safety standards as municipal-system water. But while the EPA mandates daily monitoring of public drinking water for many chemical contaminants, the FDA

Liza Gross is a former copy editor for *Sierra Magazine*, for which she wrote this article in 1999. She now works at the Public Library of Science as a Science Writer.

Reprinted by permission from *Sierra Magazine* (May/June 1999).

requires less comprehensive testing only once a year for bottled water. Beyond that, says Crawley, the FDA "usually inspects only if there's a complaint. Yet sources of bottled water are just as vulnerable to surface contamination as sources of tap water. If the spring is near a cattle farm, it's going to be contaminated."

5   Let's assume your store-bought water meets all the safety standards. What about the bottle? Because containers that sit for weeks or months at room temperature are ideal breeding grounds for bacteria, a bottle that met federal safety standards when it left the plant might have unsafe bacteria levels by the time you buy it. And because manufacturers aren't required to put expiration dates on bottles, there's no telling how long they've spent on a loading dock or on store shelves. (Bacteria also thrive on the wet, warm rim of an unrefrigerated bottle, so avoid letting a bottle sit around for too long.) But even more troubling is what may be leaching from the plastic containers. Scientists at the FDA found traces of bisphenol A-an endocrine disruptor that can alter the reproductive development of animals-after 39 weeks in water held at room temperature in large polycarbonate containers (like that carboy atop your office water cooler).

Wherever you get your water, caveat emptor should be the watchword. If you're simply worried about chlorine or can't abide its taste, fill an uncapped container with tap water and leave it in the refrigerator overnight; most of the chlorine will vaporize. If you know your municipal water is contaminated, bottled water can provide a safe alternative. But shop around. The National Sanitation Foundation (NSF) independently tests bottled water and certifies producers that meet FDA regulations and pass unannounced plant, source, and container inspections. And opt for glass bottles-they don't impart the taste and risks of chemical agents and they aren't made from petrochemicals.

☞ LOTTERYVILLE, USA ☜

Kim Phillips-Fein

First appeared in the *Baffler* no 7 (1995)

W hat would you do if you won a million dollars? Forget the revolution: This is your ticket to the Kingdom of Freedom. No matter how many hours you log in at a fast-food restaurant or behind a secretary's desk, it's unlikely you'll ever save enough to buy a house or have credit-card companies calling up with prime offers, let alone get your hair and thighs to look like those of the Aaron Spelling actresses who tantalize you every Monday and Wednesday night. Dream a little dream . . . for Parisian vacations, little gifts for the wife, a chance to start the business you've always dreamed of, a chance to give it all away. The classless society is happening right now, at a party at a mansion in Beverly Hills. And a lottery ticket might buy you an invitation.

In Grand Crossing, a neighborhood on the South Side of Chicago, the average monthly spending on the lottery is $60 per household. Grand Crossing lies just west of the South Shore neighborhood, home of the much-lauded community-development-oriented South Shore Bank. Jeffery Boulevard, the busy commercial thoroughfare where the Bank's headquarters are located, is lined with thriving small businesses—hair salons, pizzerias, Black-owned clothing stores. But traveling from South Shore to Grand Crossing you pass a boarded-up apartment building, an abandoned grocery store, a deserted TV repair shop. A little bit further and you come to Stony Island Avenue. The businesses here are distinctly different than on

---

Kim Phillips-Fein is a professor of American History at the Gallatin School of Individualized Study at New York University. She wrote "Lotteryville, USA" for the *Baffler*, a journal of political and cultural criticism, and it was later anthologized in *Commodify Your Dissent: Salvos from The Baffler*.

Reprinted from *Commodify Your Dissent: Salvos from The Baffler* (1997), W. W. Norton & Company.

Jeffrey—there's a Checkers, a Church's Fried Chicken, a Burger King; a neighborhood has started to become a ghetto. Next to a shuttered bar there's an ad for a pawn shop—"Need Cash Fast? Top Dollar for Broken Gold." Go under the highway that passes over the neighborhood; you'll find a sudden proliferation of storefront churches one of which, the House of Deliverance, has obviously been abandoned. At Cottage Grove there's a Currency Exchange and a store that advertises itself as selling liquor—and, as an afterthought, food. Beyond, there's nothing but ramshackle buildings, no businesses as far as the eye can see. Only the passing of an occasional bus reminds you that you're connected to the rest of the city.

Compare Grand Crossing to Bronzeville, the famous *Black Metropolis* described in 1945 by St. Clair Drake and Horace Cayton, with its "continuous and colorful movement" among locally owned businesses. A neighborhood, a city, is a concentration of people, goods, money, drawn in from the hinterlands; if much of this abundance is collected only to be dispersed again, a sizable portion remains and circulates within the closed system of the city. Drake and Cayton describe the neighborhood's policy wheels, illegal private precursors to the lottery, which were run by primarily Black syndicates—the white mob took them over during the fifties—and were ways of amassing capital within the community, of making sure a few people would have enough money to support local businesses and even invest. As a way of redistributing money within the neighborhood, policy wheels didn't work too badly. It's not a coincidence that policy has been replaced by the lottery just as the local department stores and restaurants have been replaced by Burger King.

A monthly average of $4.48 is spent on the lottery per household in Flossmoor, Illinois, a wealthy suburb where the average income is $117,000 a year. In Posen, Illinois, a poor suburb where average household income is $33,000, the monthly average is $91.82. Although people of all incomes play the lottery, and the indigent, of course, can't afford to spend much, it remains overwhelmingly true that lottery players, like the policy wheel players of the past, are overwhelmingly poor. But in every way the lottery serves a wholly different function than its predecessor. On the one hand, it scrapes up revenue for starved state coffers. On the other, it inoculates the urban poor with a stiff ideological dose of eternal possibility and personal mobility. The one thing it does *not* do is collect money for local investment.

In an era when Enterprise Zones and tax cuts for businesses are all that is offered to heal the wounds of the cities, the lottery is America's perverse way of dealing with poverty and ignoring the plight of its urban poor.

5   Lotteries are part of a long and vigorous tradition in American life, going back to the colonial period when lotteries were used to amass funds for the construction of many of the hallmarks of colonial architecture—the Harvard and Yale campuses, Fanueil Hall[1] —and even for getting supplies to Revolutionary troops. During the nineteenth century, private lotteries took in millions of dollars; the last of these, a fabulously corrupt money-making machine in Louisiana, was shut down in 1896. Yet even after the last of the official lotteries was shut down, illegal wheels continued to turn great profits, and instant sweepstakes à la Publisher's Clearinghouse took the place of the lottery among the law-abiding—especially when times got rough.

The lottery came back as a tool of public finance in the late sixties and early seventies. Today, thirty-nine states have lotteries. After a few years of slow growth between 1975 and 1980, the Illinois lottery exploded: ticket sales climbed from 98 million in 1980 to 1.5 billion in 1990. Your lottery dollar breaks down like this: about 50 percent goes back in payoffs, 40 percent goes to the Common School Fund, 5 percent goes to commissions for lottery vendors, and 5 percent goes to operating the lottery. The transfer to the school fund in 1994 was $552,111,416. Of course, it's something of an accounting fiction to say that the lottery made half a billion dollars for the school fund—if the money hadn't come from the lottery it would have had to come from somewhere else in the tax structure. A more accurate way to put it might be to say that the lottery saved local property owners half a billion dollars.

State revenues shouldn't be thought of as absolute figures: the crucial question about state taxes isn't whether they're "high" or "low," but who pays them. Since every state gets its revenue from somewhere, the important question is which part of society is expected to foot the bill, and looking at the tax bill of an individual or the amount of revenue collected from a single source transforms taxes from a political matter into one of bookeeping. Tax structures, as Orange County, California,[2] is reminding the world, are ways of distributing financial power. For example, sales taxes are regressive not only because they take a more sizable cut of a poor person's income than that of someone in the upper middle class, but because they reduce the cumulative purchasing power of working people and hence the bargaining power workers have over the economy as a whole. Tax structures also indicate the roles different parts of society play in the functioning of the state, not only a bureaucratic government in Springfield but a set of obligations connecting different parts of society. The lottery is perhaps unique in that it is one of the few revenue sources that applies solely to poor and working people and doesn't affect business or property owners at all. In this it seems closer to pre-Revolutionary France, a system in which peasants picked up the brunt of the Crown's bill, than to the United States before the progressive income tax. To the policy wonk it may seem absurd to bring up feudalism in a discussion of taxes, but the comparison is more appropriate than it might seem. "Regressivity" is usually used to describe a state revenue source that exacts a larger proportion of a poor person's income than that of a rich person. However, many common state revenue sources—like excise taxes on cigarettes and the lottery—go farther than this: they take a larger *absolute* amount from the poor than the well-off, while other kinds of tax relief programs give businesses industrial parks and factory buildings at outrageous discounts.

Despite its vast ghettos, in Chicago the poor are easy to forget. Wealth is everywhere, as immanent and unreachable as the spires of the Loop seem from the South Side—a fairy city, forever hovering out of reach. Money hangs over the city like an unfulfilled promise, beckoning in the department stores, the glass skyscrapers, the taxicabs, a whiff of expensive perfume. "Get from Grand Boulevard to Easy Street," read a lottery advertisement put up in Chicago's poorest neighborhood a few years ago. "This could be your ticket out." Lottery stories sometimes eat up fifteen minutes of a half-hour news program; the ubiquitous pot of Illinois State Lottery gold at the end of a rainbow sits in the window of liquor stores all over the South Side. The message blares from the newspapers that print winning numbers, "hot" numbers, "overdue" numbers, from the hysterical screams of winners on TV. Anyone can be a millionaire. You gotta play to win. Everybody gets another chance.

A chance for what? Lottery marketing firms such as Scientific Games—which make millions from state contracts—devise scenes of wealth so surreal that they seem like Donald Trump's[3] nightmares. An ad on the New York City subway a couple of years ago showed a throne room in an island mansion, the turquoise waves of some tropical sea visible through a window behind a velvet throne; a middle-aged man in tattered bathrobe with glasses and slippers sat reading the paper while a small poodle stood at attention before him, a peculiar mixture of suburbia and imperial Russia. Yet Chicago's Kimbark Liquors, a little Hyde Park establishment that serves the South Side, sells 2,700 tickets the day before a $20 million drawing, and the purchasers don't seem to be thinking about poodles to wait on them. "It's just a dream, something to think about before you fall asleep, something to take your mind off its everyday hassles," says Larry, a salesman at Kimbark. What people think of when they play the lottery doesn't seem to be the fancy cars, the racks of CDs, the fabulous new house, the private jet; not the freedom that comes with unlimited consumption, but instead the quieter comfort of financial security, a security that is no longer obtainable through work. A middle-aged Black man at Kimbark who plays twenty dollars worth of tickets every day says that if he wins he'll go to Georgia, where it's warm. An older woman tells me she'd just like to pay off her bills. Mike Lang of the Illinois Lottery says, "Winners often buy a new car, not a Ferrari but a Buick or Cadillac." It's not being a millionaire that people long for, it's simply not being poor any more.

10   Statistically speaking, nobody ever wins the lottery. The chance 10 of picking 6 random numbers out of 54 is one in 12,913,582. Philosophers of capitalism from Adam Smith to Milton Friedman have long been perturbed by the phenomenon of people playing a game they ought to know they can't win. But sneering at the lottery as "a tax on the ignorant," claiming that people who play the lottery are poor fools, deluded and uneducated, manipulated into buying false promises of wealth, fame, and glory, is an attempt to bypass the possibility that maybe poor people actually have a good understanding of what their life chances are; maybe lottery players are *right*. At issue here is not the lottery per se but the chance of personal mobility, the question of where you can get ahead in life by saving up money; the lottery should make sense to anyone for whom the answer is nowhere. Lottery tickets aren't like investments in the stock market; they are tickets to a dramatically different kind of life, the kind of life you'll never be able to save up to just by working nine to five.

In fact, the lottery is a perfectly rational investment for a person facing a lifetime of drudgery and uncertainty. The dictums of the economists—that saving can ultimately buy you a better life, that accumulation toward re-investment ought to be the practice of any rational utility-maximizer—fail to take into account that money means one thing for the rich and quite another for the poor. Poor people's money doesn't work right. It doesn't save, it doesn't accumulate, it doesn't invest. For most people, money is simply a means to an end, a way to get food, clothing, shelter, and a little TV on the side. It gets traded in, given away, stolen, lost. Elusive and slippery, you can't put it somewhere it will stay—like a house or a pension plan—until you can make the down payment. The working man's purchasing power is just the boss's variable capital so the saying goes. To compare the cash under the mattress of the poor to the investments of the wealthy is to postulate a continuum where there is in fact a radical break.

As the progression from Bronzeville to Grand Crossing indicates, what makes a ghetto a ghetto is not so much a lack of money but the lack of institutions in which money can collect. With no local businesses through which to circulate, the green stuff disappears from poor neighborhoods into the cash registers of the few remaining chain supermarkets. It goes to the makers of Olde English 800,[4] to the tobacco millionaires, the fast-food chain owners, the landlords in the suburbs, the currency exchanges. The lottery is hardly unique in siphoning money out of a poor community—compared with most businesses that "serve" the poor it looks almost innocuous. If the model for the lottery isn't Robin Hood, it's not quite Ronald Reagan either—it robs the poor to give to the school system. That it goes to the state is perhaps a sign of how desperate state governments are for revenue, but for the players it's no different than other systems that suck their money away. To refer to the lottery as a swindle or a cheat on the poor ignores the basic truth about being poor, which is that you get cheated all the time.

Yet there is a lucky winner. The lottery is perhaps the most painless and narrow form of redistribution, taking money from the poor to enrich one of their own. While the lottery may, in a sense, be rational for the individual, it is clearly irrational for the class. Rather than simply manipulating ignorance, the lottery teaches a sly lesson: For people in desperate situations, fantasy is the answer. Reinforcing the message of personal mobility, lottery playing teaches that you're on your own, that organization and politics are loser's games. Unlike the liquor salesmen or absentee landlords, the lottery sells a vision of the future—a future imagined in terms of an unchangeable class system. The poor donate money to make a poor person rich, at which point that person and their newfound wealth pack up and move out. And the rich pay nothing for this self-containing system of political quiescence—in fact, they get a tax cut.

When people are laid off, budgets are tight, crime is rampant, and social dislocation is the norm, a microeconomic model explaining why this is the best of all possible worlds can't be far behind. The early 1980s found a new theoretical model afoot in the antiseptic world of sociologists and political scientists that suggested that a city is not an economic unit in its own right, much less a place where people work and live, but rather a "service provider"—a place offering skyscrapers, office buildings, three-martini lunches, shoeshine boys. The earliest theorizers applied rational choice theory to urban life: People shop for cities the way one might look at a J. Crew catalogue, ultimately selecting the town with the ideal mix of services and taxes for them. Later academics contented themselves with explaining the only important thing—why cities should be prostrate and powerless vassals before the lord of corporate money. Since attracting big business to the city, where it will create jobs and pay (some) taxes, is by definition good for all the members of the city, it follows that all responsible city policies aim to attract private capital, with tax breaks, infrastructure, and perks like free electricity. Cities should compete for the privilege of housing the headquarters of Sears, the factories of U.S. Steel. And any microeconomist can tell you what the result of all this competition is—a better deal for the consumer.

Debates in academia rage—do "incentives" actually attract business to an area? How much do taxes matter? *What does business want?*—questions that business publications happily answer. The *Site Selector Handbook*, for example, is quite straightforward on this intricate and difficult subject. In a recent article called "Incentive Lures: Firmly Embedded in the Location Equation," the president of a Colorado economic development council says, "I'd have to say incentives are brought up in discussions of prospects virtually 100 percent of the time today." Voltaire[5] is brought in to defend the practice: "A little evil is often necessary for obtaining a great good." And the states and localities whip themselves into masochistic lathers to demonstrate that they provide a perfect setting for *your* company. "To say our state is 'pro-business' is a little like saying the Sistine Chapel[6] is 'kinda pretty,'" reads an ad for North Carolina, touting the state's right-to-work law, its balanced budget, and its favorable bond rating. An ad for the Gateway Area, towns in Northern Illinois, Southern Iowa, and Northern Missouri, goes even farther, advertising the "Nordic stock" of the locals—"A Work Force that Earns Its Pay"—who, despite their Old World work ethic of "not just accepting hard work, but taking pride in it," come for lower wages than any workers in the surrounding cities. No sassy Black folk in Southern Iowa, no sir!

A state budget is a tricky thing to unpack, containing such oddities in its murky depths as a steep sales tax on illegal drugs so that drug dealers can be busted for tax evasion, and sales tax exemptions for all kinds of goodies ranging from manufacturing equipment to semen used for the artificial insemination of livestock. But a number of things are unmistakably clear about the lottery and the Illinois tax structure—the state has one of the highest sales taxes in the nation (6.25 percent) and one of the lowest income taxes (a flat tax of 3 percent; of the seven states with flat taxes, only Pennsylvania's is lower). The lottery, which makes up 5 percent of total state revenue, grosses about 15 times the tax on real estate transfers ($28 million a year), about 5 times the tax on corporate franchises ($93 million a year), and is gaining apace on the corporate income tax ($851 million a year). In fact, total state revenue from all forms of gambling—riverboats, the racetrack, bingo, and the lottery—now exceeds the corporate income tax, at $864 million a year. ("A tantalizing source of revenue," reads a brochure from the Comptroller's office.) When you look at the lottery and gambling alongside the variety of other revenue sources that fall most harshly on the poor—steep taxes on cigarettes, on liquor, and sales taxes—it seems evident that Illinois wants to increase taxes on working-class people, while easing up on corporations and their rich employees. But what else can they do? Chicago can't move, capital can. Rather than enact new income taxes Illinois has decided to soak the poor.

While urban governments kow-tow to capital, local property owners have staged semi-revolts at any hint of increased property taxes, leaving cities and states with a vacuum where there should be revenue. Public goods and services are needed to attract businesses and investors, yet cities keep trying to undercut each other, each offering a better deal, lower taxes, more freebies, more docile workers. The "populist"-conservative ethic of personal responsibility and lower welfare payments dovetails nicely with the businessman's dream of a "flexible" labor market and a proliferation of low-wage workers—workers whose pockets can be picked, at least in the short run, to make up for the dwindling piles of gold in state coffers. The only thing cities have plenty of these days is poor people. And the lottery is a way of exploiting that human resource, the one taxable group in a state that won't move out and whose numbers are growing.

A British academic named Barbara Goodwin has written extensively about an imaginary "just society," which is organized around a mechanism called the Total Social Lottery. The lottery, held every five years, will determine which job you have, where you live, who has children, who governs. Every citizen will receive a basic social minimum—food, health care, a place to live—and all other income will be randomly redistributed every five years in Lifestyle Packages, which include random amounts of cash. The first question my friends in the primitive 1990s have about this society is not about its instability or lack of flexibility, but whether they would have to be treated by an untrained dentist every five years. While it's similar to the kind of fantasy kids dream up in the backseat during a long car ride, Goodwin's utopia sheds a little light on our own "meritocratic" society and the dozens of belief-systems, from Andrew Carnegie's benevolent social Darwinism[7] to the ramblings of Murray and Herrnstein,[8] it has spawned in self-defense. The basic assumptions Goodwin makes about the lack of connection between the social importance of work and the size of one's income may not be so far from the mark. After all, the function of many jobs may have more to do with social discipline and profit-making than with the social importance of the work itself; people who work at McDonald's don't make hamburgers as much as they make money for the people who own the fast-food chain.

There's a strong tendency among lottery players to use numbers that have personal or numerological meaning, which are invariably random numbers in genesis—birthdays, for example, are perhaps the most random numbers of all. Numbers can have occult meanings as well—for example, 769 equals death, which for some reason makes it a lucky number. Images in dreams have numerical meaning; "abdomen" is 28-33-54, according to some dream-book publications, and "accident" is 4-31-50 if you witness one, 1-37-50 if you're in one. Other players seek order in absolute randomness; thousands of Illinois players let the Quick-Pick random-number generator pick their numbers for them. The world is moved by strange forces, irrational passions, dreams, and the randomness of birth, and wealth is largely a matter of chance, luck, and the uncontrollable variable of life-choices dictated by who your parents are. While this emphasis on the blind hand of fate, which causes some people to be born rich and others poor, may obscure the logic of a social system that keeps them that way, it poses a direct challenge to any perceived link between wealth and morality, between intellect and income, between productive power and money.

20   Because the real lucky breaks don't have anything to do with chance, America is a country built on a gamble; from the flash in the pan of the California Gold Rush to the liar's poker[9] of the stock exchange, the American myth crowns those who risk all for precious metals, mouthwatering spices, towering condominiums. Chicago is a city of dreams, of elaborate fantasies, settled in a mad rush of real estate speculation, prospering in a financial heyday spent trading the prices of fictional bales of wheat. Yet speculation and lucky breaks, whether those of the explorer or the junk bond trader, hide a curious balance of power; Chicago's futures market was possible because of the railroads built with Eastern capital, the financial wizards of the eighties can fall back into the wide open arms of the federal government. Who will the winners be when Mayor Daley talks of bringing riverboat gambling to Chicago—the out-of-work steelworker who makes a killing at the casino, or the downtown property owner who faces a tax hike if the boats don't open soon?

The peasants pay taxes while the noblemen joust; the unproductive economy feeds off an abundance of frustrated hopes. Instead of coming to grips with the harsh realities of poverty and urban decay, our empty cities exist in a hazy dream of riches. The lottery doesn't solve the problems of the city or cure the plight of the poor, and the lottery's fog of fantastical riches can't survive forever in the harsh reality of ghetto life—which, if nothing else, may mean that someone else will have to subsidize the school system. The answer lies in the very bond the lottery tries hardest to break—the bond of solidarity, whether of class or of neighborhood or, finally, among cities. Imagine a kind of union of cities, a political unit that refused to compete for companies, instead working as a group to lay down terms for business—adequate wages for workers, laws mandating that a company remain in a given location for a specified number of years, consideration for the urban environment—rather than allowing business to lay down terms for them. The ideology of the lottery is the ideology of competition, in which each man is for himself and only one wins. Yet the only way cities can hope to win in the future is through solidarity. To get from Grand Crossing to Easy Street, cities will have to do better than the lottery—it's a loaded gamble, a fixed game, a bet which only capital can win.

End Notes

1. Eighteenth-century Boston landmark noted as a venue for free speech and political discussion.
2. Wealthy Los Angeles suburb that went bankrupt in 1994 through complex financial speculations.
3. Flamboyant New York real estate magnate and Atlantic City casino owner known for his ostentatious buildings.
4. Brand of beer.
5. French philosopher and literary figure (1694–1778), author of *Candide*.
6. Major chapel of the Vatican, famous for its frescoes by Michelangelo.
7. Nineteenth-century theory that Darwin's "survival of the fittest" applies to people in groups.
8. Authors of *The Bell Curve* (1994), which argued that intelligence is not equally distributed among ethnic groups, with blacks having less than whites or Asians.
9. High-stakes card game full of bluffing; also the title of a 1989 book about rampant Wall Street speculation.

✑ COULD YOU LIVE WITH LESS? ✑

Stephanie Mills

1 Compared to the lifestyle of the average person on Earth, my days are lush with comfort and convenience: I have a warm home, enough to eat, my own car. But compared to most of my urban American contemporaries, I live a monastically simple life.

Since 1984 I've made my home outside a small city in lower Michigan, where the winters are snowy but not severely cold. My snug 720-square-foot house is solar- and wood-heated. No thermostat, just a cast-iron stove. There's electric lighting, indoor plumbing, a tankless water heater, a secondhand refrigerator and range—but no microwave oven, no dishwasher, no blow-dryer, no cordless phone. My gas-sipping compact station wagon has 140,000 miles on it and spreading patches of rust. I've never owned a television set. My home entertainment center consists of a thousand books, a CD-less stereo system, a picture window and two cats.

Part of the reason I live the way I do is that as a freelance writer, my income is unpredictable and at best fairly unspectacular. Thus it behooves me to keep in mind the difference between wants and needs. Like all human beings, I have some needs that are absolute: about 2,500 calories a day, a half a gallon of water to drink, a sanitary means of disposing my bodily wastes, water to bathe in, something muscular to do for part of the day and a warm, dry place to sleep. To stay sane I need contact with people and with nature, meaningful work and the opportunity to love and be loved.

I don't need, nor do I want, to complicate my life with gadgets. I want to keep technology at the periphery rather than at the center of

Stephanie Mills is a freelance writer living in Northern Michigan. She has written many essays and four books about ecology. She wrote this essay in 1998 for *Glamour*.

my life, to treat it like meat in Chinese cuisine—as a condiment rather than as a staple food. Technology should abet my life, not dominate or redefine it. A really good tool—like a sharp kitchen knife, a wheelbarrow or a baby carrier, all of which have been with us in some form for thousands of years—makes a useful difference but doesn't displace human intelligence, character or contact the way higher technologies sometimes do. Working people need the tools of their trade, and as a writer, I do have a fax, but I've resisted the pressure to buy a personal computer. A manual typewriter has worked well for me so far. Noticing that the most computer-savvy people I know are always pining for more megabytes and better software, I've decided not to climb on the purchasing treadmill of planned obsolescence.

5   Doing with less is easier when I remember that emotional needs often get expressed as material wants, but can never, finally, be satisfied that way. If I feel disconnected from others, a cellular phone won't cure that. If I feel like I'm getting a little dowdy, hours on a tanning bed can't eradicate self-doubt.

Why live in a snowy region when I don't use central heat? I moved here for love several years ago, and while that love was brief, my affection for this place has grown and grown. I like the roots I've put down; living like Goldilocks, moving from chair to chair, seems like not much of a life to me.

Being willfully backward about technology suits my taste—I like living this way. Wood heat feels good, better than the other kinds. (Central heating would make my home feel like it was just anywhere.) Fetching firewood gets me outdoors and breathing (sometimes gasping) fresh air in the wintertime when it's easy to go stale. It's hard, achy work to split and stack the 8 or 12 cords of stove wood I burn annually. I've been known to seek help to get it done. But the more of it I do myself, the more I can brag to my city friends.

My strongest motivation for living the way I do is my knowledge, deep and abiding, that technology comes at a serious cost to the planet and most of its people. Burning fossil fuels has changed the Earth's climate. Plastics and pesticides have left endocrine-disrupting chemicals everywhere—in us and in wildlife, affecting reproductive systems. According to Northwest Environment Watch in Seattle, the "clean" computer industry typically generates 139 pounds of waste, 49 of them toxic, in the manufacture of each 55-pound computer.

I refuse to live as if that weren't so. In this, I'm not unique. There are many thousands of Americans living simply, questioning technology, fighting to preserve what remains of nature. We're bucking the tide, acting consciously and succeeding only a little. Yet living this way helps me feel decent within myself—and that, I find, is one luxury worth having.

ꝏ DOG DAYS ꝏ

Richard C. Morais

While no one was watching, Fluffy crept up onto the bed and ate the bank statement. Fortunes are getting both spent and made in the care and feeding of pets.

By the Numbers

In 2002, 64 million homes, or 62% of all U.S. households, had a pet, up from 52 million in 1988. That adds up to:
65 million dogs
78 million cats
26 million small animals and reptiles
17 million birds
192 million fresh and saltwater fish
According to the Census Bureau, there are just 72 million children under the age of 18 in America.

Michael Bannerman, 44, is a hardened criminal defense attorney on Philadelphia's mean streets, but when it comes to his dog, Laci, a 2-year-old Chinese Crested Powder Puff, the man is mush. Bannerman spent $1,500 last year on his lapdog, buying her everything from canine jewelry to handmade dog beds. Laci's 11 outfits include a mock fur coat and a motorcycle jacket. Fifteen different styles of leash hang from the front door of his home and the floor is littered with dog toys. "Laci is definitely a kid substitute," says

---

Richard Morais is a Senior Editor for *Forbes* magazine, for which he wrote this article. In addition to being an accomplished journalist, he has written several novels and an autobiography of Pierre Cardin.

Reprinted by permission from *Forbes*, 173:13 (June 21, 2004).

Bannerman, engaged to a woman who owns five cats. "I got Laci after I turned 40 and realized I wasn't going to have kids."

Bannerman's feelings for Laci aren't an aberration but part of a social trend. Not only do more people keep an animal, but a lot of people treat them royally. Pet spending in the U.S. is estimated at $34 billion this year, up 68% net of inflation over the past decade. It's an industry apparently immune to recession and, though once thought to be mature, it is expected to grow more than 6% a year for years to come. Already its sales dwarf those of toys ($20 billion) and candy ($24 billion).

The fastest-growing groups of pet buyers, according to Consumer Products & Services Trend Report, are empty nesters and young professionals who postpone starting families but want a substitute.

No surprise, then, that 83% of pet owners refer to themselves as "Mommy" or "Daddy," that 66 million dog and cat owners buy Christmas gifts for their pets or that 23 million celebrate their pets' birthdays. Donald Smith, dean of Cornell University's veterinary school, knows of couples who won't fly together for fear of leaving their pets "orphans" in the event of a catastrophic event.

"I grew up on a farm in southern Idaho," says Dr. Marty Becker, 49, author of The Healing Power of Pets, "and back then dogs had a utilitarian role, to herd cows or retrieve the duck. Because they weren't neutered, they were very territorial and guarded your stuff real good. And I can remember the specific time when it changed. There was this incredible snowstorm, and I asked my dad if we could bring Luke, our black Lab, inside for the night. Luke never left. He went from the linoleum porch to the carpet, to the couch, to the bed. I witnessed, in rural southern Idaho, this migration of biblical proportions."

The migration continues: Ashley Cofone owns a pair of West Highland White Terrier puppies called Fred and Barney. Cofone, 28, calls the dogs "my boys" and confesses she has spent $2,000 on them at Pooch, a classy pet boutique in Philadelphia, buying, for example, winter outfits. Whoops, the dogs have outgrown the stuff. Not only does she have to buy them new wardrobes, she says, but she is moving into a townhouse, and she's told her decorator she wants to custom order Fred's and Barney's beds so they are color-coordinated with the house's decor.

Lots of cute pet products and ideas originate with entrepreneurs. But two bigger retailers are consolidating a fragmented business: $3 billion (revenue) PetsMart and $1.7 billion Petco Animal Supplies.

Together their market capitalizations total $6.3 billion. The third force is Wal-Mart.

Petco, founded in San Diego in 1965, was built into a national chain by a former Toys "R" Us executive who acquired more than 20 regional companies in rapid succession during the 1990s. Today the company has 670 stores. Sales have been compounding at a 15%-a-year rate for the last five years, while the gross profit margin (sales less cost of goods and occupancy) has risen from 27% to 33%. Earlier this year Petco dropped $45 million, plus lease obligations, to cherry-pick 20 stores from Office Depot, part of a plan to reach 1,250 outlets. There's room to grow: Pet superstores still account for only 15% of the market.

Other big players are scrambling to get at the teat: Hartz Mountain is remaking itself. In the last few years Switzerland's Nestlé spent $10 billion acquiring Ralston Purina, while Procter & Gamble has spent $2.3 billion on Iams/Eukanuba. Harley-Davidson, Burberry, Old Navy, Gucci, Paul Mitchell and Omaha Steaks—these and more have pet-related products. Starwood Hotels & Resorts Worldwide has announced pet-friendly policies at its Sheraton, Westin and W Hotel chains. Its pet package includes oversize pet pillows, doggie robes and turndown treats.

The revolution in expectations is evident at two Petco stores. An old unit in King of Prussia, Pa. is a dimly lit cinderblock warehouse with birdcages and dog food unimaginatively stacked against the walls. Petco's remodeled Union Square store in New York City is, in contrast, a cheery place full of glassed-in aviaries, eerie landscapes filled with green tree frogs and veiled chameleons, and cat-and-dog adoption charities. A customer's request—"Where are the pee-pee pads?"—sends an employee scurrying among the racks, while colorful banners remind Petco's loyalty club members that they get a bag of free food after every ten purchases. Saltwater fish and tanks are big sellers. "People in the city like expensive things that look good," explains store manager Matthew Everding. "It's easy money."

Later this year Petco is to unveil yet another store-remodeling scheme, this one including a "pet spa" complete with grooming and "doggy day care." "It will be," says James Myers, chief executive of Petco, "for the customer who might be working late and wants a place where his dog can go and play with other dogs, that's better than leaving it alone." Same sort of upgrade on the shelves: James Cunningham, who runs privately held Harper Pet Products of Bedford, Ill., a producer of rawhide chews, says Petco is the Bloomingdale's of pet supplies. It added his line of expensive, flavorful and thicker hides from U.S. cattle to the cheaper and thinner hides from Brazil.

20   Braxton's Animal Works, a third-generation retailer in Wayne, 20 Pa., has survived the superstore invasion. This Main Line favorite has doubled its sales the last decade, to nearly $3 million, selling rawhide "lollipops" for 29 cents; Grandma Newton's baked-fresh-daily dog biscuits—including canine cannoli—for $1.19 each; and elegant headstones customized with a deceased pet's name and ranging in price from $43 to $270 (plus shipping). But there is also a serious theme to Braxton's shelves: health-related products aimed at extending the lives of pets.

Which leads to the question: Is this all really about the owners, or the animals?

"People keep projecting onto their animals how they feel about themselves and what they want in their own life," says Myers. "The premium-pet-food craze very much reflects human interest in better diets. Animals are now eating better, have a better coat and are slightly longer-lived." According to Packaged Facts, premium pet food accounts for 37% of a $13 billion market and should hit 41% by 2008. A decade ago premium food was a tiny segment of a market dominated by cheap supermarket brands like Alpo and Friskies.

John and David Braxton recall that in their father's time only vets prescribed specialty foods for pets; today their store is filled with chewable vitamin supplements and various specialties for dogs with "sensitive skin" or "sensitive stomachs." The premium-pet-food manufacturers—such as Colgate Palmolive's Hill's Science Diet and P&G's Iams and Eukanuba—are selling foods that claim to help cats pass hairballs; reduce dogs' tartar, plaque and bad breath; control osteoarthritis; control diabetes and kidney disease and generally aid in "senior care."

"There's an insatiable appetite today for new benefits and concepts," says Robert Devine, chief executive of Hartz Mountain. His next focus: interactive toys that relieve the boredom and stress of pets left alone when owners are at work. Already a DVD, made by the Couch Potato Kitty, lets cats chase virtual squirrels, jump at seagulls and paw at fish on the TV screen.

25   For veterinarians, these are busy days. According to a study by Pet 25 Business, cat owners made an average of 1.6 vet visits apiece in 2000;

just two years later they had upped their visits to 2.3 a year. The average amount dog owners spent out of pocket on a vet visit increased from $196 to $263 during the same period.

"We are getting closer to human medicine," says Barry Stupine, director of the Matthew J. Ryan Veterinary Hospital of the University of Pennsylvania, where revenues have jumped 88%, to $16 million, in the last five years. The hospital is, for example, a leader in cat kidney transplants, a $7,500 procedure paid out of pocket. Who would do such a thing? "I've got a waiting list of people," says Stupine. At Cornell between $2,600 and $3,000; diode laser therapy for glaucoma, $400 to $600 per eye.

The industry is ripe with opportunities not yet seized. In Sweden 57% of dog owners have pet insurance. In the U.S., where a pet's cancer treatment can cost $5,000, only 2% of dog owners buy pet health insurance. Vendors in Europe include big companies like German's Allianz. In the U.S. the market is the province of small insurers like Pet Assure and Lincoln General Insurance.

Lawyers have not missed this turn. Robert Vetere, director of the American Pet Products Manufacturers Association, warns of a push in state legislatures to shift the human-pet relationship away from property rights and toward something eerily akin to legal guardianship. It's happening in Rhode Island and California, for example—and could open up legal liabilities in pet adoptions and sales.

For now, though, it's a love affair. Says Dr. Becker: We leave work feeling like a "human piñata, beat but not quite broken, and the last thing we want to see is more people. You never know how your partner is going to be. You certainly don't know if your kids are even going to acknowledge you're home. But by God, that dog is going to treat your homecoming like the Second Coming of Christ."

LOVE AND LOSS

On Natural Death

Lewis Thomas

Lewis Thomas (1913–1994), a physician, scientist, educator, and literary figure of some repute, was born in Flushing, New York. Educated at Princeton (B.S.), Harvard Medical School (M.D.), and Yale (M.A.), Lewis established a career in medical research, education, and administration. He was dean of the School of Medicine at New York University and at Yale University and director of the Sloan-Kettering Cancer Center in New York City. Throughout his career in medicine, Thomas published extensively. Although much of his writing appeared in specialized scientific journals, his love of language and his ability to communicate complex topics to general readers enabled him to gain an appreciative lay audience. Thomas's recognition as a skilled and enjoyable essayist began in the mid-1970s, when a series of columns written for the venerable New England Journal of Medicine *and collected in the book* Lives of a Cell *won the National Book Award for Arts and Letters. Thomas assembled four additional collections of his essays, including* The Medusa and the Snail *(1979), from which this essay was taken. In this essay, Thomas argues that nature makes death easier by providing dying creatures with a respite from pain.*

1   There are so many new books about dying that there are now   1
special shelves set aside for them in bookshops, along with the
health-diet and home-repair paperbacks and the sex manuals.
Some of them are so packed with detailed information and step-by-step instructions for performing the function that you'd think this was
a new sort of skill which all of us are now required to learn. The

strongest impression the casual reader gets, leafing through, is that proper dying has become an extraordinary, even an exotic experience, something only the specially trained get to do.

Also, you could be led to believe that we are the only creatures capable of the awareness of death, that when all the rest of nature is being cycled through dying, one generation after another, it is a different kind of process, done automatically and trivially, more "natural," as we say.

An elm in our backyard caught the blight this summer and dropped stone dead, leafless, almost overnight. One weekend it was a normal-looking elm, maybe a little bare in spots but nothing alarming, and the next weekend it was gone, passed over, departed, taken. Taken is right, for the tree surgeon came by yesterday with his crew of young helpers and their cherry picker, and took it down branch by branch and carted it off in the back of a red truck, everyone singing.

The dying of a field mouse, at the jaws of an amiable household cat, is a spectacle I have beheld many times. It used to make me wince. Early in life I gave up throwing sticks at the cat to make him drop the mouse, because the dropped mouse regularly went ahead and died anyway, but I always shouted unaffections at the cat to let him know the sort of animal he had become. Nature, I thought, was an abomination.

Recently I've done some thinking about that mouse, and I wonder if his dying is necessarily all that different from the passing of our elm. The main difference, if there is one, would be in the matter of pain. I do not believe that an elm tree has pain receptors, and even so, the blight seems to me a relatively painless way to go even if there were nerve endings in a tree, which there are not. But the mouse dangling tail-down from the teeth of a gray cat is something else again, with pain beyond bearing, you'd think, all over his small body.

There are now some plausible reasons for thinking it is not like that at all, and you can make up an entirely different story about the mouse and his dying if you like. At the instant of being trapped and penetrated by teeth, peptide hormones are released by cells in the hypothalamus and the pituitary gland; instantly these substances, called endorphins, are attached to the surface of other cells responsible for pain perception; the hormones have the pharmacologic properties of opium; there is no pain. Thus it is that the mouse seems always to dangle so languidly from the jaws, lies there so quietly when dropped, dies of his injuries without a struggle. If a mouse could shrug, he'd shrug.

I do not know if this is true or not, nor do I know how to prove it if it is true. Maybe if you could get in there quickly enough and administer naloxone, a specific morphine antagonist, you could turn off the endorphins and observe the restoration of pain, but this is not something I would care to do or see. I think I will leave it there, as a good guess about the dying of a cat-chewed mouse, perhaps about dying in general.

Montaigne had a hunch about dying, based on his own close call in a riding accident. He was so badly injured as to be believed dead by his companions, and was carried home with lamentations, "all bloody, stained all over with the blood I had thrown up." He remembers the entire episode, despite having been "dead, for two full hours," with wonderment:

> *It seemed to me that my life was hanging only by the tip of my lips. I closed my eyes in order, it seemed to me, to help push it out, and took pleasure in growing languid and letting myself go. It was an idea that was only floating on the surface of my soul, as delicate and feeble as all the rest, but in truth not only free from distress but mingled with that sweet feeling that people have who have let themselves slide into sleep. I believe that this is the same state in which people find themselves whom we see fainting in the agony of death, and I maintain that we pity them without cause. . . .In order to get used to the idea of death, I find there is nothing like coming close to it.*

Later, in another essay, Montaigne returns to it:

> *If you know not how to die, never trouble yourself, Nature will in a moment fully and sufficiently instruct you; she will exactly do that business for you; take you no care for it.*

10   The worst accident I've ever seen was in Okinawa, in the early   10 days of the invasion, when a jeep ran into a troop carrier and was crushed nearly flat. Inside were two young MPs, trapped in bent steel, both mortally hurt, with only their heads and shoulders visible. We had a conversation while people with the right tools were prying them free. Sorry about the accident, they said. No, they said, they felt fine. Is everyone else okay, one of them said. Well, the other one said, no hurry now. And then they died.

Pain is useful for avoidance, for getting away when there's time to get away, but when it is end game, and no way back, pain is likely to be turned off, and the mechanisms for this are wonderfully precise and quick. If I had to design an ecosystem in which creatures had to live off each other and in which dying was an indispensable part of living, I could not think of a better way to manage.

Questions on Meaning

1. What does Thomas believe happens to pain when someone or something is dying? What does he feel is the "usefulness" of pain?
2. What is the main difference between the death of Thomas's elm and the death of a field mouse in the jaws of his cat?
3. What is the effect of peptide hormones—endorphins—on cells?

Questions on Rhetorical Strategy and Style

1. Describe how Thomas analyzes the process of pain blocking that he suggests might prevent the mouse from suffering. How does he relate this process to dying in general?
2. Reread the descriptions of Montaigne's near-death experience and the MPs' deaths. How do these narratives support Thomas's argument? Do you find any weaknesses in these examples?
3. Explain how Thomas injects dry humor into his writing. What is the impact of this satire?

Writing Assignments

1. Describe a person you know who has endured severe pain, faced a near-death experience, or died. Explain why the person's experience with pain and dying does or does not support Thomas's contention that pain likely shuts off at death.
2. People often joke that the best way to die might be to be "hit by a truck," meaning be killed instantly and without warning. Do you agree? Write an essay on the perfect way to die. How much knowledge of your impending death would you want? What would you want to do before you died? What role would pain and suffering, hospitals and drugs play?

CLOSE TO HOME; WHEN LIFE'S PARTNER COMES PRE-CHOSEN

Shoba Narayan

We sat around the dining table, my family and I, replete from yet another home-cooked South Indian dinner. It was my younger brother, Shaam, who asked the question. "Shoba, why don't you stay back here for a few months? So we can try to get you married."

Three pairs of eyes stared at me across the expanse of the table. I sighed. Here I was, at the tail end of my vacation after graduate school. I had an Air France ticket to New York from Madras in 10 days. I had accepted a job at an artist's colony in Johnson, Vt. My car, and most of my possessions, were with friends in Memphis.

"It's not that simple," I said. "What about my car . . .?"

"We could find you someone in America," my dad replied. "You could go back to the States."

They had thought it all out. This was a plot. I glared at my parents accusingly.

Oh, another part of me rationalized, why not give this arranged-marriage thing a shot? It wasn't as if I had a lot to go back to in the States. Besides, I could always get a divorce.

Stupid and dangerous as it seems in retrospect, I went into my marriage at 25 without being in love. Three years later, I find myself

---

Shoba Narayan is a native of India who spent many years in the United States before returning to Bangalore, India, where she currently resides. She has a Master's degree in Journalism from Columbia University and works as a freelance writer. This article was written for the *New York Times* in 1995.

---

relishing my relationship with this brilliant, prickly man who talks about the yield curve and derivatives, who prays when I drive, and who tries valiantly to remember names like Giacometti, Munch, Georgia O'Keeffe and Kandinsky.

My enthusiasm for arranged marriages is that of a recent convert. True, I grew up in India, where arranged marriages are common. My parents' marriage was arranged, as were those of my aunts, cousins and friends. But I always thought I was different. I blossomed as a foreign fellow in Mount Holyoke where individualism was expected and feminism encouraged. As I experimented with being an American, I bought into the American value system.

10   I was determined to fall in love and marry someone who was not   10
Indian. Yet, somehow, I could never manage to. Oh, falling in love was easy. Sustaining it was the hard part.

Arranged marriages in India begin with matching the horoscopes of the man and the woman. Astrologers look for balance and cyclicality, so that the woman's strengths balance the man's weaknesses and vice versa. Once the horoscopes match, the two families meet and decide whether they are compatible. It is assumed that they are of the same religion, caste and social stratum.

While this eliminates risk and promotes homogeneity, the rationale is that the personalities of the couple provide enough differences for a marriage to thrive. Whether or not this is true, the high statistical success rate of arranged marriages in different cultures—90 percent in Iran; 95 percent in India, and a similar high percentage among Hasidic Jews in Brooklyn and among Turkish and Afghan Muslims—gives one pause.

Although our families met through a mutual friend, many Indian families meet through advertisements placed in national newspapers.

My parents made a formal visit to my future husband's house to see whether Ram's family would treat me well. My mother insists that "you can tell a lot about the family just from the way they serve coffee." The house had a lovely flower garden. The family liked gardening. Good.

15   Ram's mother had worked for the United Nations on women's-   15
rights issues. She also wrote humorous columns for Indian magazines. She would be supportive. She served strong South Indian coffee in the traditional stainless steel tumblers instead of china; she would be a balancing influence on my youthful radicalism.

Ram's father had supported his wife's career even though he belonged to a generation of Indian men who expected their wives to stay home. Ram had a good role model. His sister was a pediatrician in Fort Myers, Fla. Perhaps that meant he was used to strong, achieving women.

Nov. 20, 1992. Someone shouted, "They're here!" My cousin Sheela gently nudged me out of the bedroom into the living room.

"Why don't you sit down?" a voice said.

I looked up and saw a square face and smiling eyes anxious to put me at ease. He pointed me to a chair. Somehow I liked that. The guy was sensitive and self-confident.

20 He looked all right. Could stand to lose a few pounds. I liked the 20 way his lips curved to meet his eyes. Curly hair, commanding voice, unrestrained laugh. To my surprise, the conversation flowed easily. We had a great deal in common, but his profession was very different from mine. I learned that he had an M.B.A. from the University of Michigan and had worked on Wall Street before joining a financial consulting firm.

Two hours later, Ram said: "I'd like to get to know you better. Unfortunately, I have to be back at my job in Connecticut, but I could call you every other day. No strings attached, and both of us can decide where this goes, if anywhere."

I didn't dislike him.

He called 10 days later. We talked about our goals, dreams and anxieties; we argued over which was the best pizza place in New York, and we teased and joked with each other. He never seemed to be in a rush.

"What do you want out of life?" he asked me one day. "Come up with five words, maybe, of what you want to do with your life." His question intrigued me. "Courage, wisdom, change," I said, flippantly. "What about you?"

25 "Curiosity, contribution, balance, family and fun," he said. In 25 spite of myself, I was impressed.

One month later, he proposed and I accepted. Our extended honeymoon in Connecticut was wonderful. On weekends, we took trips to Mount Holyoke, where I showed him my old art studio, and to Franconia Notch in New Hampshire, where we hiked and camped. We huddled under the covers on rainy summer days and caught up on each other's lives.

It was in Taos, N.M., that we had our first fight. Ram had arranged for a surprise visit to the children's summer camp where I used to work as a counselor. We visited my old colleagues with their Greenpeace T-shirts and New Age commune mentality. Ram, with his clipped accent, neatly pressed clothes and pleasant manners, was so different. What was I doing with this guy? On the car trip to the airport, I was silent. "I think, perhaps, we might have made a mistake," I said slowly. The air changed.

"Your friends may be idealistic, but they are escaping their lives, as are you," he said. "We are married. Accept it. Grow up!"

He had never spoken to me this harshly before, and it hurt. I didn't talk to him during the entire trip back to New York.

That fight set the pattern of our lives for the next several months. In the evening, when Ram came home, I would ignore him or blame him for bringing me to Connecticut. Half-heartedly, I searched for a job and mutely handed him the rejection letters. He would hold me, whispering soothing words, but I was too depressed to care about it. Or him.

Two years into our marriage, something happened. I was ashamed to realize that while I had treated Ram with veiled dislike, he had always tried to improve our relationship. I was admitted to the journalism program at Columbia, where, at Ram's insistence, I had applied.

Falling in love, for me, began with small changes. I found myself relishing a South Indian dish that I disliked, mostly because I knew how much he loved it. I realized that the first thing I wanted to do when I heard some good news was to share it with him. Somewhere along the way, the "I love you, too" that I had politely parroted in response to his endearments had become sincere.

My friends are appalled that I let my parents decide my life partner; yet, the older they get the more intriqued they are. I am convinced that our successful relationship has to do with two words: tolerance and trust. In a country that emphasizes individual choice, arranged marriages require a familial web for them to work. For many Americans that web doesn't exist. As my friend Karen said, "How can I get my parents to pick out my spouse when they don't even talk to each other?"

⌒ THE RIGHT HAND OF THE ⌒ FATHER

Thomas Lynch

I had an uneventful childhood. Added to my mother's conviction that her children were precious was my father's terrible wariness. He saw peril in everything, disaster was ever at hand. Some mayhem with our name on it lurked around the edges of our neighborhood waiting for a lapse of parental oversight to spirit us away. In the most innocent of enterprises, he saw danger. In every football game he saw the ruptured spleen, the death by drowning in every backyard pool, leukemia in every bruise, broken necks on trampolines, the deadly pox or fever in every rash or bug bite.

It was, of course, the undertaking.

As a funeral director, he was accustomed to random and unreasonable damage. He had learned to fear.

My mother left big things to God. Of her nine children, she was fond of informing us, she had only "planned" one. The rest of us, though not entirely a surprise—she knew what caused it—were gifts from God to be treated accordingly. Likewise, she figured on God's protection and, I firmly believe, she believed in the assignment of guardian angels whose job it was to keep us all out of harm's way.

But my father had seen, in the dead bodies of infants and children and young men and women, evidence that God lived by the Laws of Nature, and obeyed its statutes, however brutal. Kids died of gravity and physics and biology and natural selection. Car wrecks and

---

Thomas Lynch is a funeral director at Lynch and Sons in Milford, Michigan. He writes poetry and essays, and has published several books, including *The Undertaking*, from which this essay was excerpted.

Reprinted from *The Undertaking: Life Studies from the Dismal Trade* (1998), Penguin Putnam Inc.

measles and knives stuck in toasters, household poisons, guns left loaded, kidnappers, serial killers, burst appendices, bee stings, hard-candy chokings, croups untreated—he'd seen too many instances of His unwillingness to overrule the natural order, which included, along with hurricanes and meteorites and other Acts of God, the aberrant disasters of childhood.

So whenever I or one of my siblings would ask to go here or there or do this or that, my father's first response was almost always "No!" He had just buried someone doing that very thing.

He had just buried some boy who had toyed with matches, or played baseball without a helmet on, or went fishing without a life preserver, or ate the candy that a stranger gave him. And what the boys did that led to their fatalities matured as my brothers and sisters and I matured, the causes of their death becoming subtly interpersonal rather than cataclysmic as we aged. The stories of children struck by lightning were replaced by narratives of unrequited love gone suicidal, teenagers killed by speed and drink or overdosed on drugs, and hordes of the careless but otherwise blameless dead who'd found themselves *in the wrong place at the wrong time.*

My mother, who had more faith in the power of prayer and her own careful parenting, would often override his prohibitions. "Oh, Ed," she would argue over dinner, "Leave them be! They've got to learn some things for themselves." Once she told him "Don't be ridiculous, Ed," when he'd refused me permission to spend the night at a friend's house across the street. "What!" she scolded him, "Did you just bury someone who died of a night spent at Jimmy Shryock's house?"

He regarded my mother's interventions not as contrarieties, but as the voice of reason in a world gone mad. It was simply the occasional triumph of her faith over his fear. And when she stepped into the fray with her powerful testimony, he reacted as the drunken man does to the cold water and hot coffee, as if to say, *Thanks, I needed that.*

But his fear was genuine and not unfounded. Even for suburban children who were loved, wanted, protected, doted over, there were no guarantees. The neighborhood was infested with rabid dogs, malarial mosquitoes, weirdocs disguised as mailmen and teachers. The worst seemed always on the brink of happening, as his daily rounds informed him. For my father, even the butterflies were suspect.

So while my mother said her prayers and slept the sound sleep of a child of God; my father was ever wakeful, ever vigilant, ever in earshot of a phone—in case the funeral home should call in the middle of the night—and a radio that monitored police and fire calls. In my childhood I can recall no day he was not up and waiting for me and my siblings to awaken. Nor can I remember any night I lived at home, until I was nineteen, when he was not awake and waiting for our arrival home.

Every morning brought fresh news of overnight catastrophes he'd heard on the radio. And every night brought stories of the obsequies, sad and deliberate, which he directed. Our breakfasts and dinners were populated by the widowed and heartsore, the wretched and bereft, among them the parents permanently damaged by the death of a child. My mother would roll her eyes a little bit and dole out liberties against his worry. Eventually we were allowed to play hardball, go camping, fish alone, drive cars, date, ski, open checking accounts, and run the other ordinary developmental risks—her faith moving mountains his fear created.

"Let go," she would say. "Let God."

Once she even successfully argued on behalf of my older brother, Dan, getting a BBGun, a weapon which he promptly turned against his younger siblings, outfitting us in helmet and leather jacket and instructing us to run across Eaton Park while he practiced his marksmanship. Today he is a colonel in the army and the rest of us are gun-shy.

Far from indifferent, my mother left the business of Life and Death to God in His heaven. This freed her to tend to the day-to-day concerns of making sure we lived up to our potential. She was concerned with "character," "integrity," "our contribution to society," and "the salvation of our souls." She made no secret of her belief that God would hold her personally accountable for the souls of her children—a radical notion today—so that her heaven depended on our good conduct.

For my father, what we did, who we became, were incidental to the tenuous fact of our being: That We Were seemed sufficient for the poor worried man. The rest, he would say, was gravy.

There were, of course, near misses. After the usual flues, poxes, and measles, we entered our teen years in the sixties and seventies. Pat was sucker-punched in a bar fight by a man who broke a beer bottle over his head. Eddie drove off a bridge, crashed his car into the riverbank, and walked away unscathed. He told our parents that another car, apparently driven by an intoxicant, had run him off the road. We called it "Eddie's Chappaquiddick" privy as only siblings are to our brother's taste for beer and cocaine. Julie Ann went through the windshield of a friend's car when the friend drove into a tree and, except for some scalpline lacerations and scars, lived to tell about it. Brigid took too many pills one night in combination with strong drink and what her motivation was remained a mystery for years, known only to my mother. For my part, I fell off a third-story fire-escape in my third year of college, broke several Latin-sounding bones, fractured my pelvis, and compressed three vertebrae but never lost consciousness. My English professor and mentor, the poet Michael Heffernan, was first downstairs and out the door to where I had landed. I must have appeared somewhat dazed and breathless. "Did you hit your head?" he kept asking once he had determined I was alive. "What day is it?" "Who is the president of the United States?" To assure him I had not suffered brain damage, I gave out with "The Love Song of J. Alfred Prufrock"—a moving rendition I was later told, marred only by my belching through the couplet where your man says, "I grow old . . . I grow old . . . I shall wear the bottoms of my trousers rolled." Then I puked, not from the fall but from the J.W. Dant Bourbon that was credited with saving my life. I had been sufficiently limbered up, it was reasoned, by generous doses of Kentucky sour mash, to have avoided permanent damage.

In the hospital I woke to a look on my father's face I shall always remember—a visage distorted by rage and relief, at war with itself. And by amazement at the menagerie of friends and fellow revelers who accompanied me to hospital. While Professor Heffernan could affect the upright citizen in tweeds and buttondowns, not so Walt Houston, who studied physics and comparative religion and lived most of the school year in a tree somewhere on the edge of the campus and scavenged for food scraps in the student union. Nor Myles Lorentzen, who successfully failed his draft physical after the ingestion of massive doses of caffeine—pot after pot of black coffee followed by the eating whole of a carton of cigarettes. Later, Myles would do hard time in prison for the illegal possession of marijuana. A month after his release they made possession a misdemeanor, punishable by a twenty dollar fine. Worse still, Glenn Wilson, whose only utterance after a six pack of beer was always "Far out, man!" which he would say, for no apparent reason, at the most inappropriate of times. Harmless drunks and ne'er-do-wells, my father looked suspicious of my choice of friends.

My mother thanked God I had not been killed, then fixed her eyes on me in a way it seemed she'd had some practice at—casting the cold eye of the long suffering in the face of a boozy loved one. My father had quit drinking the year before, joined A.A., began going to meetings. My brothers and I had been a little surprised by this as we had never seen him drunk before. I had overheard my mother's sister once, complaining aloud about my father's drinking. I must have been six or eight years old. I marched down to Aunt Pat's on the next block and told her outright that my father wasn't a drunk. And once, the Christmas after his father had died, I heard him and my mother come home late. He was raving a little. I thought it must be grief. He insisted the doctor be called. He said he was having a heart attack. The doctor, I think, tried to cover for him, behaved as if there was something wrong other than drink. In any case, by the time I'd taken my dive off the balcony, my father had a year's sobriety under his belt and should have been able to recognize an inebriate when he saw one. But instead of a curse, he saw blessing: his son, somewhat broken but reparable and *alive*.

Now they are both dead and I reckon a fixture in my father's heaven is the absence of any of his children there, and a fixture in my mother's is the intuition that we will all follow, sooner or later but certainly.

We parent the way we were parented. The year they began to make real sense to me was 1974. In February the first of my children was born. In June we purchased the funeral home in Milford. I was a new parent and the new undertaker in a town where births and deaths are noticed. And one of the things I noticed was the number of stillbirths and fetal deaths we were called upon to handle. There was no nearby hospital twenty years ago; no medical office buildings around town. The prenatal care was not what it should be, and in addition to the hundred adult funerals we handled every year in those days, we would be called upon to take care of the burial of maybe a dozen infants—babies born dead, or born living but soon dead from some anomaly, and several every year from what used to be called crib death and is now called Sudden Infant Death Syndrome.

I would sit with the moms and dads of these babies—dead of no discernible cause—they simply forgot to breathe, trying to make some sense of all of it. The fathers, used to protecting and paying, felt helpless. The mothers seemed to carry a pain in their innards that made them appear breakable. The overwhelming message on their faces was that nothing mattered anymore, nothing. We would arrange little wakes and graveside services, order in the tiny caskets with the reversible interiors of pink and blue, dust off the "baby bier" on which the casket would rest during the visitation, and shrink all the customs and accouterments to fit this hurt.

When we bury the old, we bury the known past, the past we imagine sometimes better than it was, but the past all the same, a portion of which we inhabited. Memory is the overwhelming theme, the eventual comfort.

But burying infants, we bury the future, unwieldy and unknown, full of promise and possibilities, outcomes punctuated by our rosy hopes. The grief has no borders, no limits, no known ends, and the little infant graves that edge the corners and fencerows of every cemetery are never quite big enough to contain that grief. Some sadnesses are permanent. Dead babies do not give us memories. They give us dreams.

And I remember in those first years as a father and a funeral director, new at making babies and at burying them, I would often wake in the middle of the night, sneak into the rooms where my sons and daughter slept, and bend to their cribsides to hear them breathe. It was enough. I did not need astronauts or presidents or doctors or lawyers. I only wanted them to breathe. Like my father, I had learned to fear.

And, as my children grew, so too the bodies of dead boys and girls I was called upon to bury—infants becoming toddlers, toddlers becoming school children, children becoming adolescents, then teens, then young adults, whose parents I would know from the Little League or Brownies or PTA or Rotary or Chamber of Commerce. Because I would not keep in stock an inventory of children's caskets, I'd order them, as the need arose, in sizes and half sizes from two foot to five foot six, often estimating the size of a dead child, not yet released from the county morgue, by the sizes of my own children, safe and thriving and alive. And the caskets I ordered were invariably "purity and gold" with angels on the corners and shirred crepe interiors of powdery pink or baby blue. And I would never charge more than the wholesale cost of the casket and throw in our services free of charge with the hope in my heart that God would, in turn, spare me the hollowing grief of these parents.

There were exceptions to the "purity and gold." Once a man whose name I remember shot his two children, ages eight and four, while their mother waited tables up in town. Then he shot himself. We laid him out in an 18-gauge steel with the Last Supper on the handles and his daughter and his son in a matching casket together. The bill was never paid. She sold the house, skipped town. I never pursued it.

And one Christmastide twin six-year-olds fell through the ice on the river that divides this town. It ran through their backyard and no one knows if they went in together or one tried to save the other. But the first of the brothers was found the same day and the next one was found two days later, bobbed up downstream after the firemen broke up the ice by the dam. We put them in the one casket with two pillows, foot to foot—identical in their new Oshkosh B'Gosh jeans and plaid shirts their mother had mail-ordered from Sears for Christmas. Their father, a young man then, aged overnight and died within five years of nothing so much as sorrow. Their mother got cancer and died after that of grief metastasized. The only one left, the twins' older brother, who must be nearing thirty now, is long gone from this place.

And I remember the poor man with the look of damage on him whose wife strangled their eight-year-old son with a belt. Then she wrote a fourteen-page suicide note, explaining why she felt her son, who had been slow to read, faced a lifetime of ridicule and failure she felt she was freeing him from. Then she took three dozen pills, lay down beside the boy, and died herself. First he selected a cherry casket and laid them out together in it, the boy at rest under his mother's arm. But before the burial, he asked to have the boy removed from the mother's casket and placed in one of his own and buried in his own grave. I did as he instructed and thought it was sensible.

So early on I learned my father's fear. I saw in every move my children made the potentially lethal outcome. We lived in an old house next door to the funeral home. The children grew up playing football in the side yard, roller skating in the parking lot, then skateboarding, riding bikes, then driving cars. When they were ten, nine, six, and four, their mother and I divorced. She moved away. I was "awarded" custody—four badly saddened kids I felt a failure towards. And though I was generally pleased with the riddance that divorce provides—the marriage had become a painful case—I was suddenly aware that single parenting meant, among other things, one pair of eyes to watch out for one's children with. Not two. One pair of ears to keep to the ground. One body to place between them and peril; one mind. There was less conflict and more worry. The house itself was dangerous: poison under every sink, electrocution in every appliance, radon in the basement, contagion in the kitty litter. Having been proclaimed by the courts the more "fit" parent, I was determined to be one.

I would rise early, make the sack lunches while they ate cereal, then drive them to school. I had a housekeeper who came at noon to do the laundry and clean and be there when the youngest came home from kindergarten. I'd be at the office from nine-thirty until four o'clock, then come home to get dinner ready—stews mostly, pastas, chicken and rice. They never ate as much as I prepared. Then there was homework and dance classes and baseball, then bed. And when it was done, when they were in bed and the house was ahum with its appliances, washer and dryer and dishwasher and stereo, I'd pour myself a tumbler of Irish whiskey, sit in a wingback chair and smoke and drink and listen—on guard for whatever it was that would happen next.

Most nights I passed out in the chair, from fatigue or whiskey or from both. I'd crawl up to bed, sleep fitfully, and rise early again.

The poor cousin of fear is anger.

It is the rage that rises in us when our children do not look both ways before running into busy streets. Or take to heart the free advice we're always serving up to keep them from pitfalls and problems. It is the spanking or tongue lashing, the door slammed, the kicked dog, the clenched fist—the love, Godhelpus, that hurts: the grief. It is the war we wage against those facts of life over which we have no power, none at all. It makes for heroes and histrionics but it is no way to raise children.

And there were mornings I'd awaken heroic and angry, hungover and enraged at the uncontrollable facts of my life: the constant demands of my business, the loneliness of my bed, the damaged goods my children seemed. And though it was anything but them

I was really angry at, it was the kids who'd get it three mornings out of every five. I never hit, thank God, or screamed. The words were measured out, meticulous. I seethed. After which I would apologize, pad their allowances, and curry forgiveness the way any drunk does with the ones he loves. Then I stopped drinking, and while the fear did not leave entirely, the anger subsided. I was not "in recovery" so much as I was a drunk who didn't drink and eventually came to understand that I was more grateful than resentful for the deliverance.

But faith is, so far as I know it, the only known cure for fear—the sense that someone is in charge here, is checking the ID's and watching the borders. Faith is what my mother said: letting go and letting God—a leap into the unknown where we are not in control but always welcome. Some days it seems like stating the obvious. Some days it feels like we are entirely alone.

Here is a thing that happened. I just buried a young girl whose name was Stephanie, named for St. Stephen; the patron of stonemasons, the first martyr. She died when she was struck by a cemetery marker as she slept in the back seat of her parents' van as the family was driving down the interstate on their way to Georgia. It was the middle of the night. The family had left Michigan that evening to drive to a farm in Georgia where the Blessed Mother was said to appear and speak to the faithful on the thirteenth of every month. As they motored down the highway in the dark through mid-Kentucky, some local boys, half an hour south, were tipping headstones in the local cemetery for something to do. They picked one up that weighed about fourteen pounds—a stone. What they wanted with it is anyone's guess. And as they walked across the overpass of the interstate, they grew tired of carrying their trophy. With not so much malice as mischief, they tossed it over the rail as the lights of southbound traffic blurred below them. It was at this moment that the van that Stephanie's father was driving intersected with the stolen marker from the local cemetery. The stone was falling earthward at thirty-two feet per second, per second. The van was heading south at seventy miles per hour. The stone shattered the windshield, glanced off Stephanie's father's right shoulder, woke her mother riding in the passenger seat and, parting the space between the two front seats, struck Stephanie in the chest as she lay sleeping in the back seat. She had just traded places with her younger brother who cuddled with his two other sisters in the rear seat of the van. It did not kill Stephanie instantly. Her sternum was broken, her heart bruised beyond repair. A trucker stopped to radio for help but at two A.M. in Nowhere, Kentucky, on a Friday morning, such things take time. The family waited by the roadside reciting the rosary as Stephanie gasped for air and moaned. They declared her dead at the hospital two hours later. Stephanie's mother found the stone in the back seat and gave it to the authorities. It said RESERVED FOSTER and was reckoned to be a corner marker from the Foster Lot in Resurrection Cemetery.

Sometimes it seems like multiple choice.

A: It was the Hand of God. God woke up one Friday the 13th and said, "I want Stephanie!" How else to explain the fatal intersection of bizarre events. Say the facts slowly, they sound like God's handiwork. If the outcome were different, we'd call it a miracle.

Or *B*: It wasn't the Hand of God. God knew it, got word of it sooner or later, but didn't lift a hand because He knows how much we've come to count on the Laws of Nature—gravity and objects in motion and at rest—so He doesn't fiddle with the random or deliberate outcomes. He regrets to inform us of this, but surely we must understand His position.

Or *C*: The Devil did it. If faith supports the existence of Goodness, then it supports the probability of Evil. And sometimes, Evil gets the jump on us.

Or *D*: None of the above. Shit happens. That's Life, get over it, get on with it.

Or maybe *E*: All of the above. Mysteries—like decades of the rosary—glorious and sorrowful mysteries.

Each of the answers leaves my inheritance intact—my father's fear, my mother's faith. If God's will, shame on God is what I say. If not, then shame on God. It sounds the same. I keep shaking a fist at the Almighty asking *Where were you on the morning of the thirteenth?* The alibi changes every day.

Of course the answers, the ones that faith does not require, and are not forthcoming, would belong to Stephanie's parents and the hundreds I've known like them over the years.

I've promised Stephanie's headstone by Christmas—actually for St. Stephen's Day, December 26th. The day we all remember singing Good King Wenceslaus. Stephen was accused of blasphemy and stoned in 35 A.D.

When I first took Stephanie's parents to the cemetery, to buy a grave for their daughter, her mother stood in the road and pointed to a statue of The Risen Christ. "I want her over there," she said, "at the right hand of Jesus." We walked across the section to an empty, unmarked space underneath the outstretched granite right arm of Christ. "Here," Stephanie's mother said, her wet eyes cast upward into the gray eyes of Christ. Stephanie's father, his eyes growing narrow, was reading the name on the neighboring grave. FOSTER is what it read. It was cut in stone.

STUDY: PEOPLE USE IM TO HOOK UP, AVOID, AND DUMP EACH OTHER

Jacqui Cheng

A recent survey has confirmed what many of us have long feared: the proliferation of instant messaging has begun to make younger generations more socially "challenged" when it comes to real-life interaction. Okay, that may be a bit of an exaggeration, but teenagers spend an increasing amount of time IMing, the second annual Instant Messaging Trends Survey conducted by the Associated Press and AOL discovered. The survey showed that teens who IM a lot are likely to be attached to a computer and multitask than their adult counterparts. Oh, and they're more likely to say things that they wouldn't otherwise say in person—bitch. (I take it back. Let's be BFF.)

"If they freak out or something, you don't see it," 17-year-old Cassy Hobert told the AP. "And if I freak out, they don't have to see it."

It seems she's not alone in wanting to avoid the messy personal aspects of communication. In fact, 43 percent of people who IM feel the same way, with 22 percent using IM to ask people out and/or accept them—another 13 percent admitted to using IMs to break up with someone. Among teens, those numbers are higher: half of girls and over a third of boys said that they use IM to say things that they're afraid to in person. "If you're face to face, you can't close out

---

Jacqui Cheng has a Bachelor's degree in Interactive Multimedia Development from Purdue University and is a writer for the online journal of technology criticism *Ars Technica*, for which she wrote this article.

Reprinted by permission of the author.

the window and disappear if you've been rejected" added 19-year-old Lewis Grove. We're sure that you have an extremely healthy personal life, Lewis.

Courtesy of Jacqui Cheng.

Note: No emo teens were hurt in this reenactment

Overall, teenagers are much more likely to use IM than adults—over half of teens use IM, compared to just one in five of surveyed adults. But when it comes to regularity, teens and adults seem to be on the same page (or at least close): about half of teens who IM log on every day, which is only slightly higher than the percent of IMing adults. However, teens tend to use IM for far longer and to send more messages than adults—roughly 10 percent of teens IM for three or more hours per day, which is twice the rate of adults. Almost a fifth of teens send over 100 IMs daily, which is triple the number for adults. (For the record, I probably sent over 100 IMs before 10:00 this morning.)

5   Both teens and adults admit to multitasking while IMing people.   5
Popular multitasking activities include checking e-mail, performing
Internet searches, and researching homework assignments (for the
kiddies). Adults also like to shop online while chatting with each
other—assuming they're not at work, of course.

"Instant messaging has made its way into so many areas of our
lives and we can now take our buddies with us wherever we go.
Whether on our mobile phones, our social profiles or on the desktop
at work, our friends, family and co-workers are right there letting us
know when they're free for a question or just to chat," said AOL
senior VP David Liu in a statement. "This survey also found that
instant messaging is truly helping people become more productive
and better manage their relationships wherever they may be."

4sure, David.